the art of being an
ELEPHANT

BARNES
&NOBLE
BOOKS
NEW YORK

TEXT AND PHOTOGRAPHS
CHRISTINE AND MICHEL DENIS-HUOT

HISTORICAL INTRODUCTION
GIANNI GUADALUPI

GRAPHIC DESIGN
PATRIZIA BALOCCO LOVISETTI

GRAPHICS
PATRIZIA BALOCCO LOVISETTI
CLARA ZANOTTI

CONTENTS

1
A female sprinkles herself with sand as she leaves the Ewaso Ngiro river in Samburu.

2-3
The head of an elderly female elephant shows through the vegetation. Elephants enter adulthood around 12 years of age and live on average to 60, a life cycle approximating ours.

4-5
Several families of elephants in the Amboseli Park spend much of the day in the marshes, where they find food and water.

6-7
Just a few weeks old, this male in the Amboseli marshes will lose his brownish hair as he grows older.

8
A Roman mosaic of an African elephant, in the Bardo Museum, Tunisia.

9
At sunset, a baby elephant searches for his mother's teats for the evening meal.

Translation
Timothy Stroud

© 2003 White Star S.r.l.
Via Candido Sassone, 22/24
13100 Vercelli, Italy
www.whitestar.it

This edition published by
Barnes & Noble, Inc., by arrangement
with White Star S.r.l.
2003 Barnes & Noble Books

Library of Congress
Cataloging-in-Publication
Data available

ISBN 0-7607-4300-2
M10987654321

Printed in Italy by Grafiche Fover, Foligno (PG)
Color separation by Fotomec, Torino

PREFACE

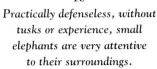

The elephant is the result of an evolutionary process that has lasted millions of years. Some think it is a vestige of prehistory, destined for extinction, like the mammoth and dinosaur. However, it is a vigorous and dynamic species that has in the past adapted to all kinds of environment. This marvel of nature has always fascinated man, and most people find it a very likeable creature. The zoologist Ian Douglas-Hamilton provides this explanation: "They are strange but intelligent creatures that resemble us very strongly in their spirit of social cohesion." Moreover, their extraordinary memory, their anatomical uniqueness, their great intelligence, and their highly developed social organization are in themselves a sufficient explanation for our fondness for them.

Elephants live in herds. In their natural environment, their nomadic life is typified by harmony and mutual support. The social balance within the family or clan is unmatched by other mammals. Female adults lead the herds with the authority conferred by a matriarchal organization. Elephants share many similarities with humans: they have the same life cycle, with the young developing in parallel to us until they reach adulthood at the age of about 17 or 18. Like us, they have a deep sense of family and death; they experience strong emotions; they can be happy and sad, aggressive and placid; they mourn the loss of their kin deeply, cry and suffer depression; and they help one another during adversity.

These huge mammals are perhaps the most studied animals in the African continent, but there is always more to be learnt. For example, it was only twenty years ago that scientists discovered that elephants are capable of communicating over large distances via infrasound.

Elephants exert great pressure on the territory in which they live, and their strength and wisdom has not prevented them from joining the list of species at risk of extinction owing to the value placed on the ivory of their tusks. Today elephants are a symbol of the African wilderness and its last open spaces. But for how much longer?

We offer heartfelt thanks to all those who have helped us to know elephants: Ian Douglas-Hamilton, Cynthia Moss, Joyce Poole, Pierre Pfeffer and Richard Leakey. We thank them too for their efforts on behalf of the wildlife of Kenya.

10
Practically defenseless, without tusks or experience, small elephants are very attentive to their surroundings.

11
At the end of the day, a young female playfully pulls her companion's tail.

12-13
A female, her youngest offspring and a slightly older elephant head toward the area where they will spend the night.

THE CURSE OF IVORY

14
An elephant, designed by Bernini but sculpted by Ercole Ferrata in 1667, supports the Egyptian obelisk in the Piazza della Minerva, Rome.

15
Lifting its trunk in greeting, proud of its caparison decorated with a royal crown, the elephant in this 18th-century engraving illustrates the letter 'E' in The Ancient Paintings of Herculaneum.

16
More realistic though earlier, this 17th century plate of a female elephant weaning her young appears in the Count de Buffon's Natural History (1749-1804).

17
This Palaeolithic rock painting is the earliest known image of an elephant. Found at Sandawe, it is now in the National Museum, Dar es Salaam, Tanzania.

In 1750 the Count de Buffon, the most influential French naturalist of the Age of Enlightenment, wrote "Currently elephants are more numerous and commonly found in Africa than in Asia; they are also less mistrustful and savage, and less solitary; it seems that they are familiar with the incompetence and lack of power of the people they have to deal with in that part of the world. Every day they come fearlessly up to their houses; they treat the Negroes with that natural and scornful indifference in which they hold all the other animals. They do not consider them as powerful or fearsome beings, but a species that only knows how to set traps, that does not dare to confront them and which has not learned the art of reducing them to slavery." In short, African elephants were unaware of the sad fate of their Asiatic cousins, which were condemned to forced labor for the benefit of man, to serve as war machines and to kill and die in battle. It is pleasant to think of pre-colonial Black Africa as an immense elephant empire that ruled over, so to speak, the innumerable tiny tribal states. Over these columns of elephants on the march used to cross from one ocean to the other by paths that led through the forest and across the savannah, heedless of human borders. Few dangers, as Buffon observed, threatened the creatures that ruled the continent at that time. Despite their cunning,

the huntsmen had only rudimentary weapons and could take only few victims. The oldest and most common method of hunting elephants was with a trap. A deep hole was dug in the ground on one of the paths the animals used to go to drink, and carefully hidden with branches and leaves, then the hunters waited for fate to take its course. Sooner or later an elephant would fall in, at which time all the hunters had to do was kill it with arrows and spears. Another method was to approach a feeding herd carefully, choose the most suitable prey (generally the fattest), then shoot it with poisoned arrows. Irritated by the small but annoying wounds, the elephant would run away from the others. After a few hours the poison would take effect and the hunters had only to follow its tracks and find their victim. The initial goal of an elephant hunt was food, for the mountain of meat it provided could feed an entire village. Like that of the rhinoceros, the skin was used to make shields, and the tail hair – which could be up to one seventh of an inch thick – to make bracelets for the women. In some tribes it was a test of courage for the bravest, to cut off the tail of a wild elephant, but this could often end in being thrown a dozen yards by a blow from the trunk or being trampled to death. Tusks were prized trophies that adorned tribal huts and the tombs of chieftains.

In 1855, as David Livingstone went down the Zambesi, he saw the grave of an important chieftain on an island surrounded by seventy enormous tusks planted in the ground with the tips facing inward. The tomb itself was covered by thirty or so elephant teeth, placed there by the chief's family. A few years earlier, in the same region, Livingstone had come across skeletons of elephants complete with tusks, a sure sign that ivory trading had not yet reached those parts. But just a decade later, a famous Big White Hunter, a Mr. Baldwin, who was following Livingstone's trail, did not see a single elephant. The only wildlife species that remained in those parts were birds. The massacre of the African fauna had begun, and the elephant was the first and most

prized trophy. Ivory was the elephants' downfall. Tusks, which nature had given them for purposes of defense, had been since antiquity a trophy so sought after that their owners had become extinct in some areas. It occurred first in the Near East, which had been one of the elephants' habitats for thousands of years. In addition to archaeological remains dating to 1500 B.C. that Sir Leonard Woolley discovered at Atchana-Alalakh, there are many literary references to the presence of elephants in Syria and Mesopotamia. For example, we know that the great Egyptian pharaoh Tuthmosis III, who reigned from 1501-1447 B.C., went off on an elephant hunt after conquering Syria. The Egyptians surprised a herd of some 120 elephants drinking, and

Tuthmosis immediately attacked them with the same fearlessness that he had shown in battle. But he found himself in serious difficulty and his charge would have ended in his death if a courtier had not intervened to cut off the 'hand,' i.e., the trunk, of the elephant that had grabbed hold of the pharaoh. Assyrian texts also refer to royal hunts. Tiglathpileser I (1115-1060 B.C.) once killed ten male elephants, and, around 840 B.C. Assurbanipal II is supposed to have killed thirty. Two hundred years later, the Asiatic elephants in Mesopotamia were extinct, not so much the result of hunts by the various Nimrods as of those by professional hunters in search of ivory. This trade was a flourishing one and Phoenician merchants exported tusks in great quantity.

18-19
An elephant in low relief on the Black Obelisk of Shalmaneser III (858-824 BC), from Mesopotamia and now in the British Museum. The elephant and the two captive monkeys are tribute being paid by Jehu, king of Israel, to the ruler of Assyria.

19 left
A small elephant figures among the Nubian tributes paid to ancient Egypt. From the rock paintings of the tomb of Rekhmire (18th Dynasty) in the necropolis of Thebes. The reproduction is taken from The Monuments of Ancient Egypt and Nubia, by Ippolito Rosellini (1832).

19 right
A small elephant statue, sadly damaged, found in Leptis Magna, on the Libyan Coast. In Roman times, this city of was one of the terminals for trans-Saharan trade, receiving elephant tusks transported by caravan.

Having disappeared in their wild state, elephants reappeared in the Near East 500 years later in their versions as tamed and military animals. At the battle of Gaugamela (the battle that put an end to the Persian Empire), Alexander the Great and his Macedonian troops saw war elephants for the first time in the ranks of the enemy. A few years later, when the conqueror had pushed into the Punjab, the rajah Porus faced Alexander with a cavalry of two hundred war elephants. However, when they were faced by the Macedonian phalanx, they backed up "like ships reversing under the power of oars," and ended up by stamping on friends and enemies alike. In spite of their unimpressive performance, Alexander thought so highly of elephants that he adopted some for his own army, but when he died in 323 B.C., his generals fought between themselves to divide up his enormous empire, setting the elephants against one another. Perdicca, the ruler of Macedonia, invaded Egypt to defeat his rival Ptolemy with a corps mounted on elephants, but his men mutinied and killed him, thereby providing Egypt with its first troop of war elephants. Ptolemy thought them an excellent weapon, as did his successor, Ptolemy II. But, unsatisfied with the number he was able, with great difficulty, to import from India, he attempted an unheard of enterprise: the domestication of wild African elephants. He sent expeditions down the Nile to Nubia to round up as many creatures as possible, and to send them to the ports of the Red Sea where they were loaded onto especially built ships. The second part of his plan was to have a number of elephant trainers sent from India whose job it would be to tame the creatures and train the Greeks and Egyptians who would ride them. The result was a company of 400 war elephants.

20 top
During his conquests of the Near East, Alexander the Great first saw war elephants in Persia, then in India. This silver decadrachma shows him on horseback, facing a war elephant. One of the elephant's riders may be Porus, a north Indian rajah.

20 bottom
Alexander's successors in Egypt, the Ptolemies, imported Indian elephants to Egypt, but they also had African ones captured in the tropics and tamed by 'experts' brought from India. This bronze statuette is in the Cairo Museum.

21
The elephants in this 15th-century miniature seem effortlessly to support huge towers filled with warriors. The miniature is from a French manuscript of the Life of Alexander the Great, by Quintus Curtius Rufus.

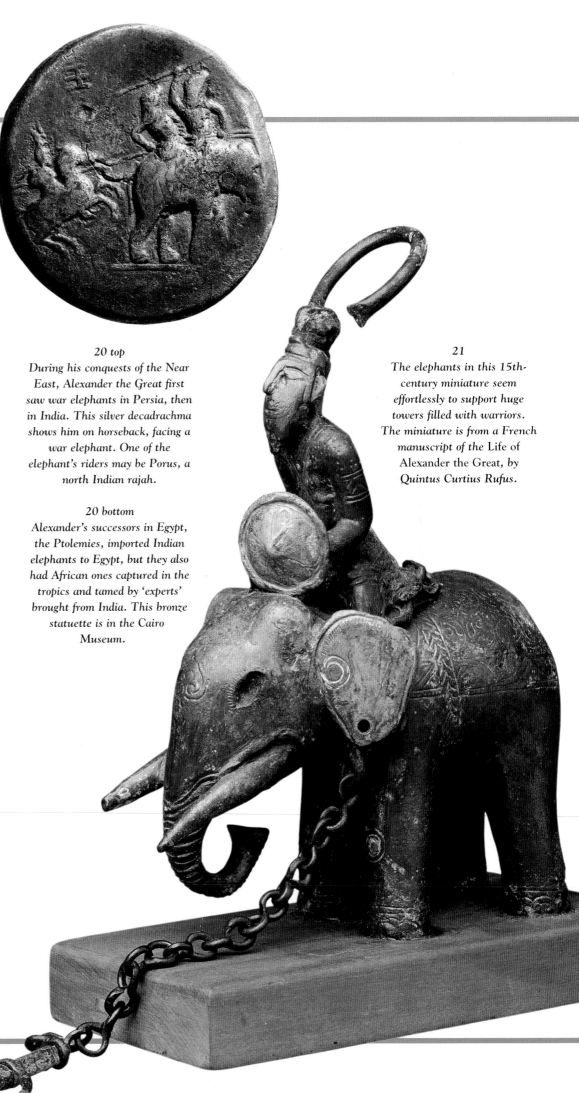

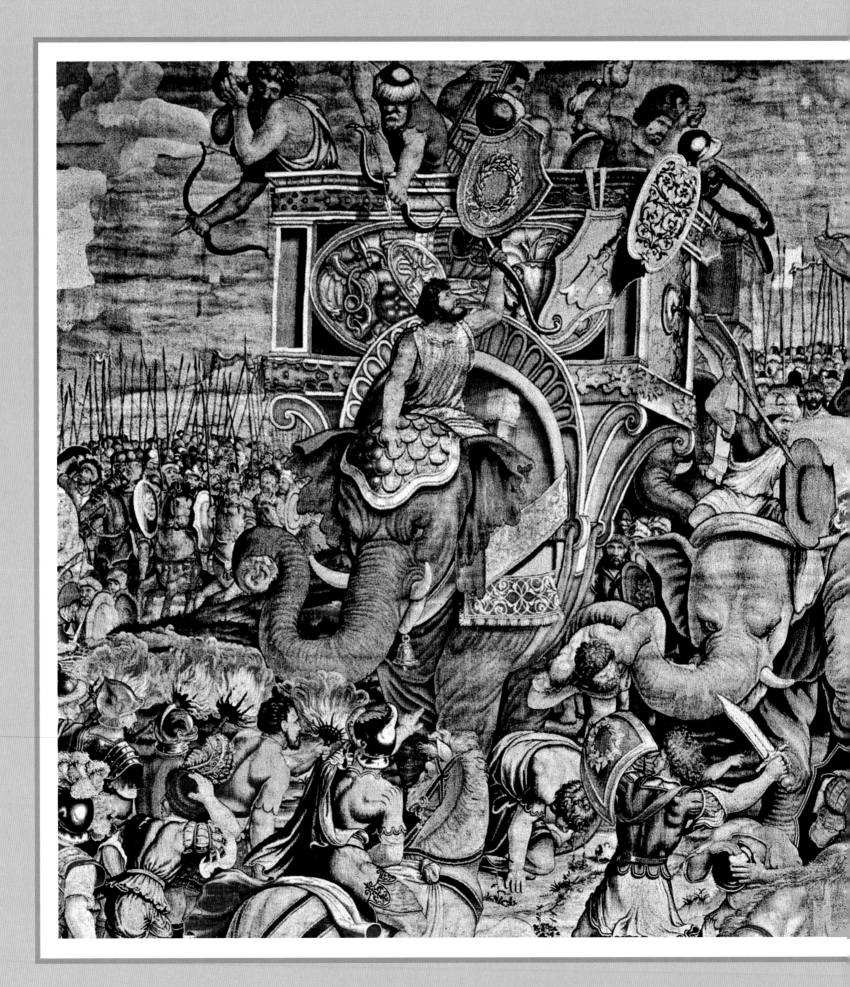

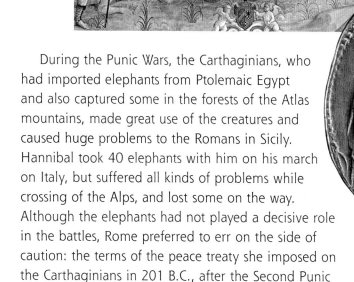

During the Punic Wars, the Carthaginians, who had imported elephants from Ptolemaic Egypt and also captured some in the forests of the Atlas mountains, made great use of the creatures and caused huge problems to the Romans in Sicily. Hannibal took 40 elephants with him on his march on Italy, but suffered all kinds of problems while crossing of the Alps, and lost some on the way. Although the elephants had not played a decisive role in the battles, Rome preferred to err on the side of caution: the terms of the peace treaty she imposed on the Carthaginians in 201 B.C., after the Second Punic War, prohibited them from owning any elephants.

The Romans had first seen elephants in 280 B.C. when King Pyrrhus of Epirus disembarked on the peninsula with the same dreams of conquest of the West as Alexander had had of the East. They were probably Indian elephants, and, at the battle of Heraclea, their trumpeting and appearance terrorized the Roman horses, which launched themselves crazily among the ranks of their own infantry, turning the situation first to confusion and then into utter tumult. In the subsequent battle of Benevento, the Romans routed the elephants by using the simple expedient of attacking while waving lighted torches. In contrast, the forty elephants with which Hannibal marched over the Alps must have been African, and the elephants used for centuries in the Roman games against beasts like tigers, bears and lions, and as jugglers and acrobats must also have come from that continent. Many sources describe elephants as being able to perform extraordinary feats of balance with their trunks. They used them to toss swords and spears up into the air and catch them again, to fight skillfully against gladiators, dance to music, walk on tightropes, or march in burlesque processions carrying, four at a time, a woman languidly stretched out on an enormous sheet.

22-23
The Carthaginians trained African elephants for use in battle. Hannibal's journey with elephants over the Alps is a famous historical episode, but some of them died on the journey. This 16th-century tapestry shows the battle of Zama (202 BC), in which Scipio defeated the Carthaginians.

23 top
Dressed as a Turk, and perched on a throne atop a seemingly bad-tempered elephant, Hannibal descends on Italy. This fresco, painted by Jacopo Ripanda, is in the Alexander Room, the Capitoline Museums, Rome.

23 bottom
The Carthaginians were proud of their elephants and often depicted them on coins. This shekel was minted in Spain by the Barca family (Hannibal's family) in the 3rd century B.C.

The ancients had immense respect for the intelligence of elephants, and attributed human capabilities to them. A great many anecdotes can be found in the works of historiographers and naturalists. According to Pliny the Elder (rather, according to the texts he consulted), elephants from Mauritania even enjoyed some sense of religiousness and worshipped the moon. At the time of the new moon, they were thought to come down from the mountains toward the River Amile. There they would purify themselves in the waters, then raise their trunks and in chorus blare out a tribute to the planet before returning to their forests, using their trunks to usher along those exhausted by the long trip. And Dio Cassius recounted what happened when Pompey organized elephants to take part in the Roman games for the first time. When the creatures understood that they had no escape from death in the ring, they attempted to move the hearts of the spectators with supplicatory behavior. Their laments seemed to express grief at the sad end that faced them, and they ran back and forth with their trunks

in the air as though to demonstrate to the gods that "they had not kept their word and taken back safely to their homeland." It seems that the normally bloodthirsty Roman people were strongly moved by the spectacle and Pompey was roundly condemned. Antipater describes two war elephants belonging to the army of Antiochus of Syria to which the king had given the names of famous Homeric heroes "because these animals feel honored by such distinctions." When the creatures had to cross a river, the first of the two, who was called Ajax and who, till that moment, had been at the head of the troop, refused to enter the swirling waters. Whereupon Antiochus harangued the creatures, promising that whichever animal crossed the river first would be rewarded. The second elephant, called Patroclus, came forward and bravely forded the river to arrive safely on the other side where he was solemnly decorated with a new silver embroidered caparison. The humiliated Ajax was degraded and, suffering from the humiliation, he let himself die of hunger within a few days.

26 top
A tiny elephant appears among the game in an 11th-century manuscript that contains the Cynegetica, a 2nd-century AD poem on hunting ascribed to Oppian. (Biblioteca Nazionale Marciana, Venice).

With the fall of the Roman Empire, Europe did not see any more elephants for several centuries and the animal passed from the realm of zoology to that of fantasy, on a par with the phoenix and the unicorn. In medieval bestiaries, the elephant was attributed with a lifespan of 300 years and its habits were tinged with Christian symbolism. According to almost all sources, when two elephants wanted to mate, "they headed east towards Paradise where the mandrake tree grew. When they reached the tree, the female ate of the fruit first and then offered it to her mate, thereby seducing him on the spot. When it was time to give birth, the female entered a lake up to her udders where she was watched over by the male, who was ready to defend her from their natural enemy, dragons. If a snake came along, the male would squash it with his foot. "An elephant's great weight prevents it from rising to its feet if it falls. Usually this happens when the animal, which has no knee joint, rests against a tree to sleep. Elephant hunters know this habit well and so partly saw through a tree so that it will fall when an elephant rests against it. The fallen elephant calls for help and immediately is joined by one or two of his companions who attempt to lift the first. However, they are unable to do so and so they both trumpet for further help.

26 bottom left
This elephant knocking down a tree appears in a manuscript of 1564, drawn up by Angelus Vergecius in Paris. It contains the text of De Animalium Proprietate, by Emanuele File, a 14th-century Byzantine poet (Bodleian Library, Oxford).

26 bottom right
The dream of every ancient farmer: a plow pulled by two strong elephants (perhaps rather too small!). The miniature is from a 15th-century codex of Pliny's Natural History (Biblioteca Nazionale Marciana, Venice).

27
The elephant in this miniature – probably Flemish – from the early16th century has vertical tusks and a very unusual spout-shaped trunk (Bodleian Library, Oxford).

28

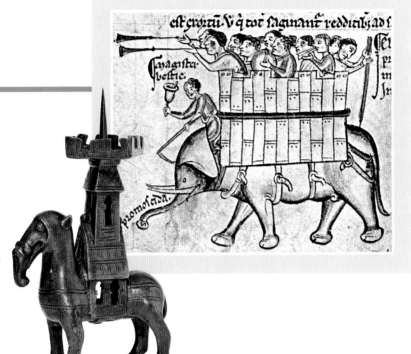

28
This elephant-borne tower brings warriors abreast the walls of a besieged city. From a 13th-century English bestiary in the Bodleian Library, Oxford.

29 top left
A bizarre elephant features in this brass candelabrum made in Germany in the 13th or 14th century (Victoria and Albert Museum, London).

29 top right
This elephant, which carries an entire tower, is incited by its bell-ringing trainer and goaded by a passenger. The 13th-century miniature is part of the Historia Maior, by the Benedictine monk Matthew Paris.

29 bottom
A horse with tusks like an elephant is portrayed in this miniature from a 15th-century manuscript in the Biblioteca Vallicelliana, Rome.

Twelve other elephants arrive but not even these are able to lift the fallen creature. They all then cry for help and a baby elephant comes along who, by placing his trunk below the stricken creature, manages to lift it up. The hide and bones of this small elephant, once reduced to ash, have the power to keep all evil or danger at bay, and perhaps even the dragon. We are therefore to recognize Christ in the baby elephant who, although being the smallest, is actually the greatest of all."

Of course, very few Europeans had ever seen an elephant, and the few elephants reached European shores produced astonishment. This happened when Pope Leo X received one as a gift in 1514 from King Manuel I of Portugal. No elephant had been seen in Italy for over a thousand years, and a great festival was organized in the creature's honor. The pope looked down from the walls of Castel Sant'Angelo on the bridge where sounds of trumpets and pipes announced the arrival of the Portuguese ambassadors wearing scarlet velvet and gold chains and riding fine horses.

The elephant was preceded by a Moor on horseback and by another on foot. A third Moor was seated on the elephant's back together with a tame leopard. After drinking from a bucket and playfully spraying the crowd, the creature kneeled before the Holy Father and saluted him with three blares from his trunk. The elephant was then housed in the Belvedere and for a long time was the favorite attraction of the Roman people.

30
An elephant hunt sketched by the explorer Samuel Baker in his diary. A group of natives (referred to as 'Arabs' in the text) attacks the animal with swords while the European's frightened horse flees.

30-31
This naïve 19th-century engraving shows a courageous female elephant. Peppered with poisoned darts, she continues to defend her calf from native hunters carrying spears.

Although Europeans were more or less ignorant about elephants, they certainly knew about ivory. This had been imported from time immemorial from North Africa, and when elephants had been hunted to extinction in the Atlas Mountains, caravans carried ivory across the Sahara. It was then that new, more efficient and more profitable means were introduced to hunt elephants in Black Africa, with the killing no longer of a single animal, but of an entire herd. For example, in equatorial regions, a group of thirty or so hunters would wait patiently until they saw a herd enter a wood or a section of a forest that could be easily surrounded and which had no water source. The followers would then begin to bang on drums and trees, blow trumpets and fire shots while the entire village of several hundred people would be called out to help surround the wood. The elephants would be too frightened to leave their cover. Then the work would begin of building a strong enclosure around the elephants, perhaps as much as a mile long, using trees and lianas. Once this was complete, the villagers could relax and wait for days, maybe weeks. Elephants have to drink a lot or they quickly lose their strength, so the hunters would then place tree-trunks inside the enclosure and fill them with poisoned water. Naturally, the elephants drank the water and the next day the slaughter of those animals still alive would begin. When around the mid-19th century Big White Hunters arrived in Africa with increasingly powerful weapons, the end of the pachyderms was in sight. All that was needed to bring them down was a single well-aimed shot. A very rough estimate has it that between 1790 and 1880 about 6,500 elephants were killed every year to produce umbrella handles and billiard balls from ivory.

*32 left
Bursting unexpectedly out of the vegetation, an elephant made even more gigantic by the artist, Emile Bayard, threatens David Livingstone, who escapes by the skin of his teeth.*

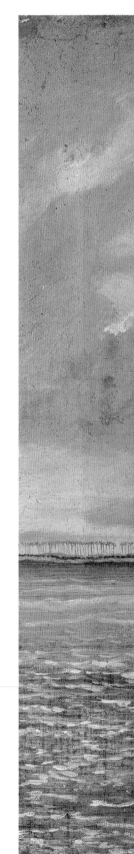

*32 right
Both Livingstone and Stanley, shown here in their famous meeting in the heart of Africa,*

were skilled hunters as well as explorers. They mention elephants several times in their memoirs as sought-after trophies.

Even for the most experienced and well armed hunters, challenging the large animals was not an encounter to be taken lightly. Probably the most famous African explorer, David Livingstone, advised newcomers to the sport to train in the following way before leaving for the Black Continent. "Whoever wishes to go elephant hunting should lay down between two railway tracks and remain there until he hears the train's whistle. When he sees the train arriving at full speed, before moving off the track, he should wait until it is just two or three steps away to know if his nerves are strong enough to face up to the giant."

It was soon discovered that elephants have a weak spot: a pack of aggressive hunting dogs can make them lose their heads. Livingstone again: "The barks of a few curs are enough for elephants to forget to defend themselves from the man who is about to attack them. In this case the only danger is that the pack of dogs, returning to the hunter, brings the beast with them." To escape from a charging elephant, white men used to hunt on horseback. Few had the courage – or fearlessness – to face them on foot, and several ended up being the victims of their prey.

William Cotton Oswell, who accompanied Livingstone on his trip across the Kalahari desert, had a frightening experience. He had earned fame as a great hunter by killing four large males in a single day, and he was admired by the locals as he did not use dogs. Once, on the banks of the Zuga, he followed an elephant into a

dense thorny thicket that lined the water. He was on horseback, following the animal along a narrow path, and just catching sight of its tail every now and then, but the elephant decided to change from being the prey to being the hunter, and turned to charge at Oswell. The Englishman did not have time to turn and flee so he tried to dismount, but the terrified horse reared and threw its rider to the ground, his face looking up toward the charging elephant. Oswell saw one of the creature's enormous feet about to stamp down on his legs so he opened them wide; at the same time he held his breath as though he might resist the pressure of another foot which he thought was about to crush him. Unbelievably, the rushing mass passed over him without touching his body and he was left unhurt.

Like Livingstone and Oswell, all the 19th-century hunters – Burton, Speke, Grant, Baker and Stanley among them – had close encounters with elephants, and to return home with the tusks of a creature they had killed personally was a point of honor. Their experiences were all similar: here, for example, is an account by Sir Samuel Baker, whose prose is the most literary of all those who wrote up their adventures.

Having sighted a herd of eleven elephants walking along the bank of the White Nile, Baker quickly entered into action as though he were in command of a military operation. "I ordered my men to run towards the heights,

Explorers shoot at an elephant from Livingstone's boat Ma Robert on the river Shiré, a tributary of the Zambesi. Thomas Baines, an artist who participated in the expedition, painted the picture in 1859.

34 top
Richard Burton (left) and John Speke (right) were hunting rivals as they explored the Great Lakes region in search of the source of the Nile. Their travel accounts contain descriptions of elephant hunts.

34-35
Facing a herd of charging elephants is the hunter's worst experience. This plate is from John Speke's book, Journal of the Discovery of the Source of the Nile, published in London in 1863.

35 left
Samuel Baker, another British explorer of Africa's Great Lakes region, was an aggressive hunter of inoffensive elephants.

35 right
Desperately searching for an escape, elephants attacked by Samuel Baker demolish a rocky bank in crossing a river to find safety in the nearby forest.

to outflank the elephants and to stop two hundred paces back … I mounted my brave horse, Gridy Grey, and … climbed the slope so as to come out downwind of the elephants. I galloped at full speed: the locals, gathered on the east bank of the river, cried out in amazement. In a few moments I reached the top of the slope about 280 to 330 feet above the elephants… Meanwhile, my soldiers, all fast runners, had scaled the heights and spread out in a long line between the slope and the river bank. Thus the elephants were surrounded on all sides … I was about to dismount, when the elephants made a half turn towards the river. I ran down to the bank but when I got there they had already crossed to the other side… It was a difficult shot as the animals had their backs to me and were perhaps more than a hundred yards away… In the end, a large male, which had come halfway up the slope, showed me his side for an instant; I shot and sent a No. 8 bullet into him. He tumbled into the river and as violent convulsions had brought him to about twenty yards from me, I finished him off with a bullet in the head.

35

"The high rocky bank had been entirely destroyed and an elephant reached the ridge. I shot with a Holland carbine loaded with three quarters of an ounce of fine powder; the recoil tore the weapon out of my hand and launched it a few yards away. The elephant fell to its knees, then, struck by a second bullet, collapsed into the river and floated away like the first." When reading accounts like this today, our admiration does not lie with the shooting skill of the hunter, but with the ingenuity the elephants showed in trying to save themselves.

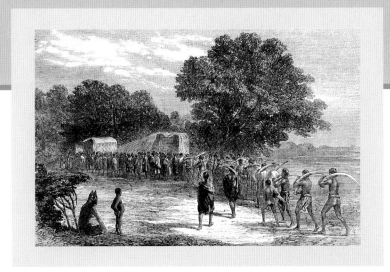

36 top
A file of porters crosses the River Tondy bearing tusks en route for the coastal ports.

36 bottom
A native hunter enters his village carrying a huge tusk from a male elephant.

The hunters who killed for sport, such as two very famous Englishmen, Cummings and Baldwin, were soon replaced by professional killers: ivory traders. Until the mid-19th century, the trading of elephants' teeth followed the routes across the Sahara and toward the Gulf of Guinea, where all the European powers, from Portugal to Prussia, had set up trading posts. Warrior tribes from the interior would bring slaves and ivory to these posts, the former sent to the American colonies and the latter to Europe. One stretch of the coast is still known as the Ivory Coast for that reason. Until that time, the main center for ivory trading had been the island of Marfim ('ivory' in Portuguese), close to the mouth of the River Senegal. Following the reduction in numbers of the elephants in western Africa and the rising demand for ivory by Europeans, a new hunting area was opened up: the unexplored heart of the continent around the Great Lakes. This was where the Arab slave merchants found most of their victims, who were then shipped down the Nile to Egypt, or sent to Zanzibar. The latter was then an independent sultanate that controlled a long stretch of the east African coast from where the slave boats left for the Islamic world. Slave and ivory trading went hand in hand: the caravans that entered the heartland of Africa to attack villages and kidnap men and women to sell in Khartoum or Zanzibar also looted the ivory reserves accumulated by the tribesmen, then they made their newfound slaves carry the ivory to the coast. It took half a century to do away with this scourge.

37 top
Where paths allowed for the use of ox-drawn carts, porters could finally relieve themselves of the heavy tusks they had been carrying.

37 center
Before leaving a village that had served as a base for raids that brought in slaves and tusks, attendants tie the tusks in pairs.

37 bottom
Other members of African caravans during the mid-19th century were female cooks (who often carried a child on their backs) and porters who carried cloth for bartering with local chiefs.

38-39
*Thousands of tusks awaiting sale in a
London dock warehouse, c. 1895.*

39
*When a white hunter killed an elephant,
the native Africans had a feast. Top
Natives slicing off prime cuts. Center and
bottom Valuable ivory en route to
collection points.*

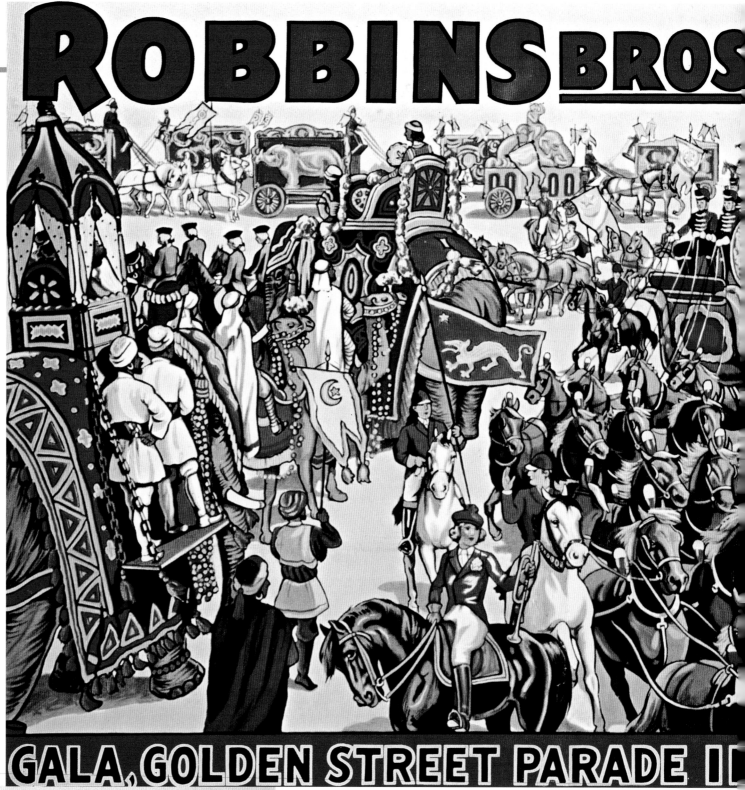

ROBBINS BROS

GALA, GOLDEN STREET PARADE II

40-41
As in ancient Rome, so in 19th- and 20th-century America. Elephants were the stars of the parade through cities where the circus was to perform. This Robbins Bros. Circus poster is in the Museum of the City of New York.

40 bottom
Taken from the 1922 album Le Cirque en images, by Juliette and Marthe Vesque, the intelligence and surprising agility of elephants allowed them to perform alone or with other animals.

CIRCUS

.oMo. PRECEDING FIRST PERFORMANCE

41 top
Elephants imitating human
behavior made them, with the
clowns, the attraction best-
loved by children. This
Ringling Bros. Circus poster is
in the Museum of the City of
New York.

In addition to the sportsmen and the ruthless ivory
hunters, other predators wandered 19th-century Africa in
search of elephants, but this time to capture them, and other
examples of wildlife, alive. These were the suppliers of zoos –
which, in the second half of the century, were opened in all
the large cities of Europe – and of circuses, whose spectacles
of trained wild animals were all the rage during the same
period and the first half of the 20th century. As in ancient
Rome, elephants once more demonstrated their extraordinary
ability as dancers, tightrope walkers and lifters of enormous
weights. Another standard act would be a group of dancing
she-elephants in colored mini-skirts (or rather, maxi-skirts)
and plumes; and the sight of an elephant's foot placed just
above the face of a lovely girl lying on the sawdust would
cause a thrill to run through the crowd.

Another elephant-related topic entered the collective
imagination of cinema-goers and adventure book readers.
This was the last myth of mysterious Africa: the Elephants'
Graveyard, the undiscovered place in the heart of the
equatorial forest where all elephants go when they feel
their end is near, to die among the bones and tusks of
their ancestors. Everyone, that is, except Tarzan, the
elephants' one human friend, who made use of them in
the jungle like a sort of taxi. He alone knew the
whereabouts of the Elephants' Graveyard, but told no one.

THE ADAPTATION OF A GIANT

42 left
A male elephant eating a favorite food, the bark and branches of Acacia tortilis (umbrella-thorn acacia). Some experts think the acacia's high concentration of calcium is an attraction.

42 right
A herd leaves the forest at the foot of Mt. Kilimanjaro, where it spent the night, and heads for the marshes.

44
Swarms of irritating mosquitoes envelop a female in Amboseli Park.

45
This male has been alarmed and is interpreting the information carried in the air. With poor eyesight, elephants depend mostly on their sense of smell.

44

THE DYNASTY
OF THE ELEPHANT

African and Asian elephants belong to the order of Proboscidea, a term that means 'hoofed creatures with trunks.' They are the last representatives of a long series of species whose original ancestor is unknown. All we are sure of is that 55 million years ago, it was still an amphibious creature. Numerous species evolved from this ancestor, with some scientists claiming three hundred or so. The first Proboscidea undoubtedly originated in Africa and southeast Asia, but later emigrated to all the continents except the Antarctic and Australia. Their proliferation and diversification has always prompted them to search for new sources of food and new habitats. They have populated the wettest forests, the driest and hottest steppes, and temperate zones with snowy winters. They even traveled to northern Europe and crossed to America when Alaska and Asia were still joined.

The earliest known Proboscideum, *Moeritherium* (whose fossils have been found in the oasis of Fayoum in Egypt, about 60 miles south of Cairo), belonged to one of the families that became extinct during the Oligocene epoch (between 40 and 25 million years ago). This solidly built creature was about the size of a dwarf hippopotamus and lived 45 million years ago in the pools and marshes of Egypt. It had neither tusks nor trunk but a long nose like that of a tapir. Its eyes

and ears were high on its head–like those of a marine mammal–so that it could remain practically submerged in the water. *Moeritherium* had no characteristics that suggested its descendants would one day be the giants of the savannah. What enables us to classify *Moeritherium* in the order of Proboscidea is the shape of the skull, and the morphology of the limbs and dentition, in particular the presence of long incisors in the shape of tusks.

The development taken by Proboscidea was gigantism. The more the various families grew in size, the shorter their necks became to be able to support their heavy heads, in particular when they had four tusks. The consequence of their bodies growing larger and their necks becoming shorter meant that they required a long and unusual appendage to ferry the food on the ground to their mouths: thus the trunk was born. With the passing of time, the jaws and incisors were transformed dramatically, passing through several unusual stages.

The strangest Proboscidea were undoubtedly those with two lower tusks in the form of a shovel or spoon. During the Pleistocene epoch, i.e., just 1 million years ago, a South American variety even had spiral tusks, and just a few thousand years ago, several dwarf families inhabited various islands around the world.

Discovery of their remains in the Mediterranean gave rise to the myth of the Cyclops. The nasal cavities of these Proboscidea opened like an eye-socket in the middle of the roundish, human-shaped skull, and this prompted the belief that the giants had just one eye.

Among the many lines of descent known, there are three main suborders: the Deinotherioidea, the extinct Mastodontoidea, and the Elephantoidea, and the main strain of the Mastodontoidea suborder known as the Gomphotheriidea.

Gomphotheriidae, which could reach a height of 10 feet, were present in Africa and Eurasia until the end of the Oligocene. Their long, slightly downward-curving tusks grew from their upper jaw and, when taken with the size of their head, could equal the length of the trunk.

Deinotherioidae did not have tusks on their upper jaw but only on the lower one. These too curved downward and in certain species even backward! The suborder disappeared about 1 million years ago.

The first Mastodontoidae appeared with the genus Paleomastodon in northern Africa at the end of the Eocene epoch (40 million years ago). They were more or less the size of today's elephants but their bodies were more solid and covered with hair. They had two slightly downward-curving tusks attached to the upper jaw, and two small horizontal tusks on the lower jaw. In this species, during the Pliocene, Miocene and Oligocene epochs (40-12 million years ago), the upper incisors grew in length while those in the lower jaw shortened until the species disappeared in the mastodons of the Ice Age.

The evolution of the Elephantoidae began 16 million years ago in the middle of the Miocene epoch. The common ancestor of the mammoth and the elephant was *Primelephas*, which had small lower tusks that slowly shortened until they disappeared, and upper tusks that never stopped growing. The chewing teeth were modified to allow mastication of hard vegetation, and the animals adapted to increasingly hostile environments and less fertile terrain.

The first mammoths lived in Africa 3 million years ago. Although they were large–up to 13 feet at the shoulder–they resembled modern Asian elephants with longer, heavier tusks. Only 120,000 years ago, some of these mastodons adapted to cold regions, with a thick reddish coat that protected the woolly mammoths from the cold and large lumps on the skull and shoulders where they could store fat to survive long periods of hardship. Their powerful tusks curved upward, which allowed them to rake the ground for grasslike plants hidden beneath the snow. The disappearance of the mammoths at the end of the last Ice Age quickly followed the equally mysterious disappearance of the Neanderthals during the Paleolithic period, roughly 40,000 years ago. Mammoths became extinct simultaneously in Eurasia and America, though indications have been found of a herd living in Siberia just 3000 years ago. The disappearance of the mammoths is not fully understood. Was it due to a sudden warming of the climate that led to profound alterations in the vegetation, or to a large natural catastrophe, epidemic, slaughter or combination of these factors?

Roughly a couple of million years ago, five species of elephants lived in the East African savannah, one of which had immense, downward-curving tusks. These elephants coexisted with strange creatures like giraffes and antelopes that both had large horns, some measuring up to 10 feet long! Most of these animals seem to have disappeared as a result of climate change. Two families of elephant survived, from which evolved the two species we know today.

The two have a number of physical differences. The genus *Elephas*, to which the Asian elephant belongs, originally evolved in Africa, but then spread to southern Eurasia. The genus *Loxodonta*, to which the

46

46
Females are smaller than males; they generally stand 10 feet tall at the shoulder, and weigh between 3 and 4 tons.

47
During the day, the young rest protected by the herd.

African elephant belongs, appeared 1.5 million years ago. Currently two subspecies exist in Africa: the forest elephant, *Loxodonta africana cyclotis*, which lives in the primary forests of central and eastern Africa, and the savannah elephant, *Loxodonta africana africana*. Even today, a good third of elephants live a separate and mysterious life in the shade of the rainforest. These creatures, still called round-eared elephants, are smaller than their savannah cousins. They do not exceed 7'10" at the shoulder, while the plains variety can reach 13 feet. Their ears are relatively smaller and rounded. These elephants are darker than their cousins, their tusks are rather straight and slim and they have a more accentuated down on their hide, concentrated beneath the chin and on the trunk. They resemble young savannah elephants, and their distinguishing features are the result of adaptation to the forest habitat.

A third variety of African elephant has often been described–the dwarf elephant *Loxodonta pumili*–which lives in primary forest and does not stand taller than 6'6" at the shoulder. They live in herds and are very aggressive; the Pygmy tribe is afraid of them. Observations in the field and examination of their skeletons has led Pierre Pfeffer, who has long studied elephants, to consider them more as young *cyclotis* (the forest elephant subspecies) that live on the edge of matriarchal groups. Other scientists are not in agreement and consider them a third subspecies.

A genetic study carried out in 1997 suggested that the forest and savannah elephants might have reached such a level of differentiation that they are now considered as separate species, as different as the lion is from the tiger. This suggestion is far from being unanimously accepted, all the more so because it was published in the same year that the elephant was declassified from having total protection in Attachment 1 of the Washington Convention (CITES: Convention for International Trade in Endangered Species). Some people interpret this claim as an attempt to create a new species excluded from the protection programs, as happened in 1976 with the dwarf blue whale. Moreover, in certain populations, for example in Garamba Park in the former Zaïre, certain elephants combine the characteristics of the two subspecies.

Elephants are the last survivors of the many subspecies of Proboscidea. To the layperson, their nearest relatives would seem to be the rhinoceros or hippopotamus, but that is not the case. In fact, they are most closely related to the manatee and dugong (both of which are Sirenids) and the hyrax, the last representative of the Hyracoidea order. This relationship seems surprising because the hyrax behaves like a marmot and the first two resemble strange, hairless pinnipeds. This is due to the fact that the classification of the species has long been largely based on descriptive anatomy. When we scrutinize these animals, which are seemingly so different, we find that the Proboscidea, Sirenidea and Hyracoidea have many points in common, in particular their dentition. The molars of the Sirenids, for example, are like those of the elephants, which become worn down and replaced by new ones that rise behind the originals and push the old ones out. The teeth of the hyrax are not like those of a rodent; the upper jaw has two incisors that have lengthened forward to become like small modified tusks. Both have pectoral udders, and their hearts are identical in structure. Furthermore, the females of the elephant species have the same type of genital orifice as the marine mammals. The hyrax has four toes on its front feet and three on the hind ones, all of which have small hoofs except for the middle rear toe, which has a claw. Special pads on the base of their feet function like suckers and allow the animal to run on steep rock walls or to move through tree branches in complete safety.

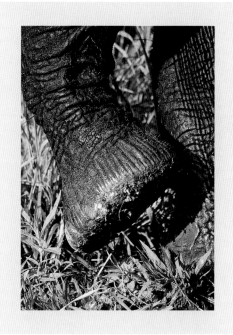

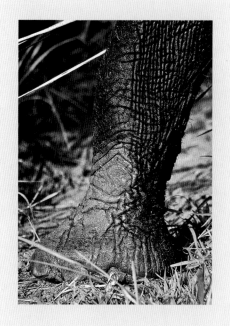

48 left and right
The heavily lined sole of the
foot is very elastic and acts as
a shock absorber. It measures
about 24 inches in diameter.
Though the skin is often
scratched, it is rare that spines
perforate it. Elephants walk
surprisingly silently.

ANATOMY OF A GIANT

The morphology of the African elephant and the originality of its physical, psychological and behavioral modifications are the result of long evolution.

The principal physical characteristic of the elephant is its gigantism. Even though another terrestrial mammal–the giraffe–exceeds it in height, the elephant is undoubtedly heavier. Only marine mammals, like the whales, rorquals and cachalots, achieve larger dimensions. The average height of a male elephant is 10'10" at the shoulder but it is not rare to find males as tall as 12'3". Males weigh on average 4.5 to 5 tons, and some rare individuals exceed 7 tons. In 1955, a male was discovered in Angola that stood 13 feet at the shoulder and weighed roughly 10 tons. The females are smaller, with a height of about 10 feet at the shoulder and a weight that ranges from 3 to 4 tons. Elephants continue to grow throughout their lives and, in consequence, the older the creature, the larger it is. However, once they have passed 25 years of age, the growth of females slows until it is almost interrupted, while males continue to grow at a perceptible rate.

Gigantism causes these creatures problems of locomotion. When a quadruped grows, its limbs must grow at a sufficient rate to support the weight of its body and enable it to walk. It has been calculated that if elephants grew to twice their height, the legs would need to be twice their current diameter and the feet would be too large to fit under the animal's body. In other words, elephants have reached the maximum stature possible for terrestrial creatures. Marine mammals have been able to develop so much because the water they inhabit frees the creatures of the force of gravity and thus removes problems caused by locomotion. During the Mesozoic era, reptiles like brachiosaurs achieved considerable dimensions (much larger than those of elephants) with legs that were proportionately shorter in relation to body size. However, this was undoubtedly linked to the fact that they lived in marshy areas that allowed them to move easily; probably they never ventured onto terra firma.

Despite their primitive appearance, the legs of elephants are the result of great adaptation; they are columnar, perfect for supporting the heavy body and their feet are examples of anatomic originality. They have conserved the five separate toes from their ancestors, which end in a small hoof or large nail. Generally the African elephant has four nails on the front feet and three behind, while the Asian elephant has five and four respectively. Not all experts agree on this and it is possible that differences exist between individuals of the same genus.

When elephants move, only the terminal phalanges rest directly on the ground, making the animal digitigrade like a dog or a horse. However, such an arrangement is definitely unsuitable to support such a heavy weight so an ingenious feature has evolved: a thick elastic cushion of fibrous sinew between the toes provides the elephant with a larger surface area on which to place its weight. This 'damper' allows the animal to adopt the gait of a plantigrade, provides it with a very elastic step and gives excellent adherence to the ground. When an elephant

49 left
Forest elephants have straighter, slimmer tusks than savannah elephants. The animals are shorter and their ears are smaller and more rounded.

49 right
The trunk has a very large number of muscles which give it mobility, strength, and surprising capabilities.

moves all his weight onto one of his legs, the cushion expands and the sole adheres perfectly to the surface of the ground, perfectly absorbing the bumps and hollows. Thus movement on inconsistent surfaces becomes possible without the risk of falling. The load-bearing surface of an elephant's feet is huge: more than 10 square feet! The division of the weight on the ground therefore does not exceed 8 pounds per square inch, and the walk of the animal, even the heaviest, is very quiet. If it were not for the sound of breaking branches, the arrival of a pachyderm could take you by surprise!

Like the fingerprints on man, the crisscross pattern of bumps and streaks left in an elephant's footprint is distinctive; it also gives an indication of the animal's age. Generally, the sole of the youngest elephants' foot has neat, exact edges, while that of the eldest elephants has more imprecise markings and worn nails. Long, oval footprints are typical of adult males, which place their hind feet almost beside their front feet as they walk. In contrast, females leave rounder prints and place their hind foot in the precise place where the front foot has just trod. A correspondence between the stature of an animal and the length of its footprints exists only in elephants less than 20 years old.

The second most important characteristic of elephants is also the most original: their trunk. In the tendency of this herbivore towards gigantism, evolution has equipped it with a tool that allows it to graze or drink without having to kneel. The trunk is capable of fulfilling more functions than can all the limbs of other mammals, including the human hand.

An elephant's trunk is the result of the lengthening and fusion of the upper lip and nose. It can reach 7 feet and is so long that, though tall, an elephant has to curl it slightly at the tip as it walks. Even so, being squashed and folded like an accordion, every now and then it extends and leaves a mark in the dust on the ground. The trunk is heavy, weighing as much as two adult men, and it is easy to understand why some elephants curl it negligently over one of their tusks from time to time. In the African elephant, the trunk's tactile tip has two lobes, in its Asian cousin, one, used like fingers, allowing the animal to pick up a leaf or seed with great delicacy. To make this possible, the lobes are endowed with a highly acute sense of touch.

This curious appendage performs a great number of functions. As a nose, it allows air to pass in toward the nasal cavity and plays an important role in smell, a sense that in all Proboscidea is much more highly developed than either sight or hearing. An elephant can smell water up to 12 miles away and the sexual receptivity of another elephant from a great distance. By moving the tip of the trunk to its mouth after touching an object, an elephant can recognize different smells. The odor of the object is passed through a small cavity in the mouth that leads to Jacobson's organ (the organ of the sense of smell) that all vertebrates share. When elephants become aware of a danger, they raise their trunks toward the wind to identify suspect scents. And the trunk helps a blind elephant move with confidence, something that astonishes scientists who have not yet shone light on all the mysteries of this wonderful organ.

50
An elephant's skin is almost 1 inch thick. Any deep wound can quickly become infected as the skin tends to scar immediately, thus preventing a wound from draining.

51
An elephant holds its head back to get the last drops of water from its trunk. To quench its thirst, it has to drink 10-20 'trunkfuls.'

Trunks also have all the capabilities of a strong limb and can uproot a large tree. Using its trunk, on average, an elephant can lift 4.5% of its own body weight which is, in the case of an adult male, up to 600 pounds but, like men, not all elephants have the same physical capacities. The trunk can also be used as a weapon capable of powerful, even mortal, blows when the creature is excited or defending itself. Many over-ambitious carnivores have been struck in this manner, then picked up and hurled to the ground. The trunk is also capable of suction, spraying, giving visual signals or a sonic alarm. It is used to stroke the partner during mating, to comfort and help other elephants and, if necessary, to punish them.

The trunk's strength and mobility are made possible by the many muscles it comprises. It is an extraordinarily complex organ composed of longitudinal and circular muscles, and by a grid of nerve fibers. Baron Cuvier calculated that an elephant's trunk might contain as many as 40,000 muscles; compare that to the human body which, in total, has no more than 693. The trunk has 6 important groups of muscles that are divided into more than 100,000 elements. The muscles of the forehead, upper lip and cheeks work together to provide surprising flexibility and mobility.

Though extraordinarily wide-ranging, the trunk is not absolutely indispensable, however surprising this may seem. Certainly, an elephant that loses its trunk is decidedly handicapped, but it is not necessarily condemned to a quick death. There are many animals whose trunk has been cut off or shortened in some manner, but they survive reasonably well. They kneel in order to eat and drink.

Evolution has provided elephants with another double-edged sword: their tusks. These overgrown incisors have no enamel except at the tip, and continue to grow throughout the animals' life. Growth occurs at the base, in the part located in the gums and in the cranium. This cavity is filled with a strongly vascularized tissue and has nerve endings. The ivory is a mixture of dentine and cartilaginous substances encrusted with calcium salts. The tusks of the elephants in Amboseli Park generally appear around the age of two years and three months, with those of the males appearing slightly before those of the females. On average tusks grow 4 inches a year in males and 3 inches a year in females, and it may happen that some animals grow more than two! The structure and consistency of ivory, like the weight and measurement of the tusks, vary depending on the climate and the animal's fodder; mineral deficiencies will have repercussions on the size and form of the tusks. The ivory of the elephants that live in very dry zones is fragile and liable to crack or break easily. This is why it is common for elephants in Etosha in Namibia to have bluntened or broken tusks. Some populations are famous for the size of their tusks, as used to be the case in the Obo triangle in the Central African Republic. Others, on the other hand, may not have any, as occurs in Zambia, Mozambique, and in Mali at the mouth of the river Niger, though this could be a godsend: as the elephants in Mali have no tusks, they have been spared by poachers.

An elephant's tusks are not necessarily the same size or shape and their degree of wear depends on whether the animal is 'right-' or 'left-handed.' Though it seems an exception, the absence of tusks in African elephants is becoming more frequent, which is quite clearly a genetic response to the preference of hunters for those with the largest tusks.

An elephant's eye, protected by long lashes, seems very small compared to the rest of its body.

The composition of the soil an elephant blows onto itself determines the color of its skin, which can appear almost white, gray, reddish or ocher.

Animals born without tusks tend to be more irascible and aggressive, probably as a direct consequence of the lack of a defensive weapon. This physical characteristic becomes hereditary.

On average, tusks weigh from 60 to 90 pounds on males and about 25 pounds on females, though the longest measured was 11'6" and weighed 230 pounds. The tusks of the famous male elephant Ahmed, from Kenya, who died in 1974, weighed in at 147 pounds each. The length of the tusks of some males can be so great that they touch the ground when the animal is at rest even when standing. In such circumstances they become a handicap and may result in the owner's becoming wounded or killed when fighting against younger males whose tusks are more manageable.

Tusks are used to rip off tree bark, unearth plant roots, dig holes in search of water or even to move obstacles. They can be fearsome weapons whether used in battle or just for intimidation, but they can become fractured if used too violently or to lift loads that are too heavy. The elephant is then subjected to intense pain that might excite it or make it dangerous. Tusks can also suffer painful tooth decay!

An elephant's skin is marked by lines and deep furrows. This conformation considerably increases the skin surface, which is especially useful in the control of body temperature. The heat that an elephant produces through its metabolic activity must be eliminated in order to keep the animal's temperature at a steady 36.5°C. This heat is lost very slowly because the animal is so robust; i.e., the ratio of skin surface to body volume is lower than it would be in

a smaller or thinner creature. Additionally, elephants do not sweat as they do not have sweat glands. Their skin, though soft, is therefore dry to the touch. The only visible glands on these mammals are the two temporal glands that lie between the eyes and ears at the sides of the head. Each gland weighs over 3 lbs and produces a strong smelling secretion that runs down the sides of the face.

The skin of the adult elephant is almost bare except for the trunk, which has some coarse hair, and the tail, which has two tufts of thick, dry and elastic hair that can reach 3 feet in length and which Africans use to make bracelets and other jewelry. This hair does not seem to have an important function for an elephant, but it is very sensitive. The hair around the eyes and ears exists for purposes of protection. Although elephants have adapted to hot regions and have a thin layer of fat beneath the skin, the animal can also stand cold temperatures and is able to inhabit mountainous regions without problems. Though the skin on the animal's back and flanks can reach a thickness of more than one inch, it is very sensitive, especially in the sun. Pricks and stings from mosquitoes, gadflies and tsetse flies can make them bleed and become very irritable.

The ears of the savannah elephant are very large, almost three times bigger than those of the Asian elephant. They nearly always have holes and notches or cuts on the edges. The veins in the ears are so prominent that they form a unique pattern that can be used to identify an individual elephant quickly and certainly. To recognize an elephant by its ears, first look at the overall shape and, if the edges do

54
An elephant's ears can measure nearly 6 feet in diameter; they perform an important role in regulating body temperature.

55
Charging is generally an intimidatory exercise: elephants usually halt a few yards from their adversary.

not have easily identified marks (which is rare), then check the pattern of the veins.

The ears can grow to a width of almost 6 feet and play a fundamental role in regulating body temperature. They are criss-crossed by a dense grid of blood vessels through which the blood circulates very quickly. The ears increase an adult elephant's body surface by almost 80 square feet and are therefore of major importance in dispersing excessive internal heat. When the ambient temperature exceeds 25°C and there is no wind, elephants use their ears as fans: the hotter it is, the harder they flap them. If there is a breeze, the elephants face into it and hold their ears outstretched in order to offer the greatest area to the wind. Elephants are also able to spray themselves with water, which is another essential means of reducing body temperature on days of intense heat. The immense ears of the savannah elephant are therefore very effective cooling elements that are indispensable to enduring hot climates. Forest elephants, which live in shady zones, have no need of such large ears and theirs are proportionately much smaller.

The elephant's enormous head is convex and regular. It has to be strong to support the weight of the trunk and tusks. Fortunately, the bones in its huge skull are spongy in structure and this lightens their mass, and the mucous-lined sinuses each have a cavity large enough to take over 5 pints of liquid. These factors ensure that the head is both mobile and large enough for the trunk and neck to enter it.

An elephant's brain weighs 9-13 pounds and is therefore 4-5 times heavier than a human brain, but like ours, it has many circumvolutions. Its size and structure suggest that elephants are able to store masses of information. The ratio of brain weight to body mass is lower than that of a gorilla or chimpanzee, but it has not yet been scientifically ascertained what influences the creature's intelligence. Scientists have tried to calculate an intelligence index based on the ratio of the weight of the brain of current and primitive mammals. So far a value of 14 has been attributed to boars, 48 to baboons, 104 to elephants, 121 to dolphins and 170 to man. This hierarchy is theoretical but approximately corresponds to intelligence tests.

At birth, a baby elephant's brain weighs 35% of those of its parents. In humans, the ratio is 26%, but in most other mammals it is around 90%. Therefore a baby elephant faces a long physical and mental development period, and this is fundamental to its intelligence. The popular saying that elephants never forget is clearly an exaggeration but, in general, their memory is excellent though it varies among individuals.

An elephant's eyes seem small in relation to its overall size, yet they measure 1.5 inches in diameter and are fringed with long lashes. They are capable of expressing all kinds of emotion: fear, boredom, derision, hostility and pugnacity. Their visual acuteness is mediocre and has been shown to be approximately equal to that of a horse. The eyes are positioned on either side of the head, which gives the animal a very wide visual field horizontally and downward. There are even blind matriarchs who are perfectly able to lead the family herd.

56
*Tusks are not always the same size. The wear
they sustain differs, depending on whether the
animal is right or left 'tusked.'*

57
*Females can be distinguished by the shape of
their forehead, which almost forms a right
angle. Those of males are more rounded.*

58

*Elephants sometimes use their trunk and tusks
to pull off tree bark.*

59

*Trunks have different functions but are foremost
for breathing (see the nostrils). The two
extensions at the tip are prehensile; they give the
trunk such dexterity that it can pick a single
blade of grass at a time.*

60

*Curled like a snake, the trunk can rest on a
tusk. This is a common position while elephants
sleep.*

61

*The trunk can serve as a human hand—and is
useful for scratching.*

ADAPTATION TO THE ENVIRONMENT

Elephants are not a vestige of prehistory that like the mammoth or dinosaur is destined to die, nor are they like certain extremely specialized animals, such as the giant panda, that depend on just one type of food. This vigorous, dynamic species has adapted to all kinds of environments, from the edges of the desert to the heart of the rainforest. Like man, elephants have not specialized to either a particular mode of living or a particular environment. Consequently, both have colonized all the habitats available to them, helped by their unusual faculty of adaptation and their intelligence.

Elephants live in African grasslands, Asian steppes and in forests (forests are undoubtedly their original habitats) but also exist in desert areas like the Skeleton Coast and Namibian Desert. They inhabit the practically desert-like El-Aagher plateau in Mauritania, where they have adapted to the meager resources and are small in size. Elephants are also to be found in Africa's mountainous country, for example, on Mt. Cameroon and Mt. Kilimanjaro, where they have been observed at altitudes over 11,500 feet, and they lived in mountainous regions in northern Africa for over 2,000 years. Contrary to appearance, they are excellent climbers on steep slopes that even man has difficulty on. The precision of their movements and their balance are surprising. When they climb a mountainside, they take the smoothest slope and create a path with their passage. Their ingenuity and intelligence allow them to perform extraordinary feats, for example, when the terrain gives them reason to doubt its trustworthiness, they advance with caution, prodding the ground constantly with their trunks or a foot to test its resistance. They have joints at the knee and ankle, which allows them to walk easily uphill, but they have difficulty on descents as their front legs are already heavily strained by supporting the weight of their head, neck, trunk and tusks. On occasions on steep descents, they may slip onto their buttocks.

In Kenya we observed elephants very carefully in three different environments. First, in Amboseli National Park, which lies in the south of Kenya at the foot of Mt. Kilimanjaro. The park measures 150 square miles and is surrounded by a reserve in which the Masai graze their herds. The periods of dry weather in this region alternate with periods of heavy rainfall, particularly in recent years. The mountain tends to attract much of the rains and the water in the park forms pools or bogs fed by very clear spring water filtered through porous lava. The subsoil in Amboseli has a strong concentration of mineral salts which means that only certain species of plants, which can put up with the salt levels, were able to survive when the main Amboseli basin dried up 5,000-10,000 years ago. Over the years, the rainwater has taken much of these salts into the subsoil, thereby allowing trees to grow on the surface, but the salts have remained in the water table and occasionally rise to the surface with the result that they kill all the vegetation.

64
In Ngorongoro Crater, many males with large tusks live in Leraï forest, characterized by tangles of 'yellow fever' acacias.

65
Elephants are very sociable animals. Here different groups happily spend their days together on the banks of the River Ewaso Ngiro.

66-67
Mt. Kilimanjaro dominates Amboseli Park and profoundly influences the local ecology. Not all the park's 700 elephants are concentrated in the central area; some migrate regularly outside, especially up on the slopes of the mountain.

The 700 elephants in the reserve are not all concentrated in the central basin at the same time. They migrate outside the park and return at will. For more than 30 years, the Dr. Cynthia Moss, an American psychologist and researcher in auditory processing and her team have been studying their biology. Other elephants live to the south of Amboseli in the forests that cover the slopes of Mt. Kilimanjaro. They neither look nor behave like the elephants in the park: they are smaller and thinner, with narrow faces, their heads are covered with hair, their ears small and triangular, their tusks lopsided, and their spiral or twisted tails rarely end in hair. The two populations are quite distinct. The one that lives on the slopes of Kilimanjaro must have remained separated from the one in the park for a sufficiently long period for their stature and appearance to be modified, perhaps to better suit life in the forests on the side of the mountain. The elephants in Amboseli are an independent population with little in common with the communities to the south and east, and for this reason they are interesting to study.

Another place that is suitable for watching elephants is the north of Kenya in the two communicating reserves of Buffalo Springs and Samburu, which are separated by the river Ewaso Ngiro. During the dry season the reserves are home to up to 700 elephants. Here the vegetation is completely adapted to the dry climate, with a great variety of species of brambles. The unsuitability of the environment to man is reflected in the name 'nyika,' which means wild or desert. In the middle of this landscape stand the ocher, brown and reddish columns built by giant termites. The immense dum palms (Hyphaene coriacea) dominate the vegetation on the banks of the rivers, and umbrella-thorn acacias are omnipresent. In the distance, large low hills form the backdrop to the green ribbon that marks the course of the river. The river is only a boundary on paper as the animals cross it with ease. Crocodiles bask in the sun on its sandy banks. It is an oasis in an arid desert.

We also spent a great deal of time with the elephants in the Masai-Mara Reserve, which forms a single ecosystem with the Serengeti and Ngorongoro National Parks in Tanzania. The reserve is composed of round hills, shrubby areas and huge expanses of grazing land dotted with the occasional acacia. It is bounded to the east by the Loita hills and to the west by the Isuria declivity. The land lies at an altitude of 5,000-8,000 feet and the temperature is mild. The river Mara and its tributary, the Talek, run all year round, and the marshes, like Musiara where the elephants live, remain wet even during the dry season. Created in 1950, the reserve was extended in 1961 and now covers 583 square miles, but only 250 of these are completely protected as Masai animal breeders live in 'temporary' villages on the other side where they graze their flocks. However, this situation is changing. Around 1,500 elephants live in the region, and they are easy to find.

68

*Outside the seasonal migration period, elephants move
daily and spend the night in the forested areas.*

69

*The matriarch of the herd leads her companions in
Indian file along paths in Samburu Reserve.*

*To scratch themselves where their trunks cannot
reach, elephants rub energetically against tree
trunks, rocks and even termite mounds.*

72 and 73
*Elephants are variable in their lifestyle and
environment: they can live in the Amboseli Park
marshes (where these pictures were taken) or on
the edges of a desert. The rain that falls on Mt.
Kilimanjaro is absorbed into the soil, but much
percolates into the wetlands and streams inside
the protected area.*

74-75
A group of lesser flamingoes explores a marsh in Amboseli, where many species of birds live. In the background, a herd of elephants proceeds quietly among other feeding birds.

76

*Elephants make a deep impact on their
environment, creating serious damage. Trees
suffer most, with their bark ripped off for food.*

77

*Vegetation around water courses depends partly
on elephants, who disperse the seeds of the
plants they eat.*

78-79

*Although elephants barely tolerate them, cattle
egrets insistently accompany the animals in
everything they do.*

80

*The early morning mists will quickly lift in the
Masai-Mara Reserve, where elephants often visit
the Musiara marshes.*

81

*A male sprays himself with dust among the
acacias at the foot of Mt. Kilimanjaro.*

A MATRIARCHAL SOCIETY

82 left
Head to head, two young elephants who have grown up together play close to their mothers inside the herd.

82 right
A typical group of savannah elephants, composed of females with their young, spray themselves with sand.

84
The matriarch who heads the herd gives the signal to march.

85
As the females and small ones march steadily toward water, they shower themselves with dust.

We have been in Amboseli for several days. We are beginning to familiarize ourselves with the different families of elephants that live in the central area of the park and to learn their habits. We are tracking one family in particular that has followed a regular schedule since we began watching them. In the early morning, we arrange ourselves in our off-road vehicle near the place that they normally come out of the acacia forest, where they spend the night. We cannot go to meet them as there are no routes through this terrain that our vehicle can negotiate. While we wait, through our binoculars we watch two solitary bulls who are advancing into the plain behind us. Eventually, a cloud of dust signals the herd's arrival. They walk quietly and slowly but with a determined gait. Leading the family is an old female, with lined skin, and long, fine tusks that curve upward slightly at the end. Behind her come several adult females accompanied by their offspring. The group is reasonably compact. Once they arrive in the grassy plain where the shrubs grow, they split up slightly as they begin to eat. We watch them move calmly from one tuft of grass to the next, eating as much as they can during the couple of hours that their meal lasts.

They then move to a dry, vegetationless piece of land where they pause to dust their heads and bodies using their trunks. In this way they turn pale gray, the same color as the terrain. The family regroups during this dust bath and some touch one another with their trunks. Some of the adults rub their heads against the shoulders of the old matriarch. She suddenly shakes her ears as a signal to the others and the group sets off, this time somewhat more rapidly. There is no time for eating. The elephants head in file toward the water in a marsh a little over a mile away. The youngsters follow as best as they can, almost running on their tiny feet. We see the bridge that allows them to cross the bog. There, another group of elephants is already drinking; further along the bank, a second group is also close to the water.

As soon as the herd nears the first group, trunks are extended to the side as a sign of greeting, but the matriarch offers only the smallest recognition and continues toward the second group. Suddenly she gives off a very loud blast from her trunk and the elephants waiting on the bank seem excited. They straighten their ears and noisily respond to her greeting. They are all dripping copiously down the sides of their heads. The matriarch increases her speed until the two groups come into contact. The elephants hoot, flap their ears and extend their trunks to touch the drips and cheeks of the others. Some females coil their trunks together whilst others cross their tusks in a noisy crush of bodies. Many animals urinate or defecate. The matriarch heads toward the eldest female in the other herd and they exchange long greetings. How long does the episode last? Perhaps only five or six minutes but it is a wonderful sight. Finally, calm returns. The females begin to drink with their young between their legs and adolescents begin to play. At this point it is difficult to know to which group the elephants belong as the two have become so mixed.

Later, all the elephants enter the marsh where they stay for a few hours, wandering among the dense vegetation. They eat for a long time but, when they emerge, it is still

86-87
The matriarch remembers the location of all the year-round water sources in the herd's territory.

hot. They wander off a few hundred yards, stop and fling dust over their backs and shoulders. A very young baby lies down but is not alone in doing so; four other youngsters sit, then roll over onto their sides. The adult females surround them to create a form of defensive barrier. Then they too begin to doze, with their trunks dangling onto the ground. Only one adolescent continues to play, messing about with a bunch of plants in the marsh, but then stops and goes and places its trunk over one of its companions. Everything is calm for about an hour but only the youngest sleep deeply. Occasionally, the female adults change the position of their trunk, rolling it up or letting it rest over one tusk. Some of the adults wave their ears and open their eyes. Finally, a small female begins to dust herself, then the others, thereby breaking the protective circle. The youngest stand up and two adolescents confront one another as the rest of the herd begins to urinate and defecate together. Then the matriarch gives off a long dull blast, flaps her ears against her neck and shoulders, then lets them drop. She starts off followed immediately by the other old female. This is the signal that everyone has been waiting for and the entire herd begins to follow. The matriarch raises her trunk to sniff the different smells. Tramping in a column of two or three together, they head toward the woods where they will spend the night.

88
The herd stops and awaits the arrival of a nearby group. In certain periods of the year, two herds may mix temporarily to form a single large group.

89
The females in a herd are related; they are sisters, cousins, aunts, mothers, etc.

THE WISDOM
OF THE MATRIARCHS

Small groups of elephants are to be seen everywhere in the savannah. The first few times, one doesn't pay much attention to the fact that generally there is no adult male among them. Some groups are as small as can be–a female with a youngster and an elder son–but, more often, they are composed of a number of females and their offspring. Field studies made during the 1960s, in particular by Ian Douglas-Hamilton, suggest that the adult females who live together are all related: sisters, aunts, cousins, mothers and daughters.

Physical contact seems to be very important in the social life of elephants. They often touch one another with their trunks, and rest against or stroke one another. During pauses on marches, they remain in formation, and, for most of the time, they carry out their activities together. All the members of the group perform the same activities together, whether it be drinking, eating or resting. Only when they feed do they tend to move away from one another, eating at up to a few hundred yards from one another. If the vegetation is thick, they stay in contact through sound signals. The females keep close guard over the young, and the group as a whole provides surveillance and education. The immature females in particular look after the smallest and this quickly creates links between animals of different ages. As one watches the

development of the families, it is easy to attribute human qualities to elephants. Tenderness and mutual help are unquestionably the first that spring to mind. Reciprocal assistance and cooperation to all the weaker members of the family–the young, the sick or the wounded–is clearly evident. If one elephant is slow to follow the group, the others wait and, if necessary, help it to progress. Dignity, compassion, curiosity, and the control they have over their own strength when playing are other characteristics. Harmony reigns in the family and there is no competition for either food or water. This accord may disintegrate if the group is struck by disorganization–due to the death of the matriarch or intensive poaching–but only males in musth will show signs of aggressiveness.

The greeting ceremonies among elephants provide the image that makes them such attractive creatures. Members of the same family greet one another often, though mostly in a discreet manner. When the members are reunited after a separation, however, their meetings are joyous affairs in the extreme. The longer the separation, the more energy and enthusiasm are shown when it ends, and the event may last ten minutes. They seem to experience a sort of joy, and this emotion plays an important role in their social system. Temporal secretions are very significant in the processes of recognition between individuals.

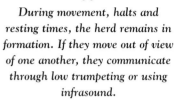

90

During movement, halts and resting times, the herd remains in formation. If they move out of view of one another, they communicate through low trumpeting or using infrasound.

An elderly female – the matriarch – leads the family. When she stops, the whole groups stops too. If she decides to start off again, she gives an energetic nod of the head and trunk and snaps her ears forward, and the whole troop sets off together. The females obey the matriarch unquestioningly. Her role is essential in the event of danger, and the others will copy her behavior whether it is to flee or to charge. When defending the young, the females generally form a circle–with their trunks beating the scrub and their heads nodding–and they let out a barrage of trumpeting. The young are hidden in the center, among the forest of adult legs.

The links between the females in a group are very strong. They do not leave one another throughout their lives, meaning that they can pass up to sixty years together. The respect for the bonds within the group and its rules is surprising.

The matriarch knows the terrain frequented by the herd perfectly; it is not a territory because it is not defended from the intrusions of other herds. She knows where to find the best fodder for the time of the year, the water points that keep their water longest during the dry season, the danger zones to avoid and the paths that her ancestors have traipsed for generations. Young females in a family learn from her knowledge and experience every day simply by following her behavior and thanks to her highly developed memory.

Compared to the society of primates, which is generally considered highly developed, what the two groups have in common is that a female passes all her life in the group of her birth whereas a male leaves it once he reaches maturity. But the large difference between the two societies lies in the relationships that an individual develops with the external world, as primates rarely have relationships outside their family. Studies in Amboseli in Kenya or in Manyara in Tanzania have shown that a given family will retain strong links with certain groups of elephants that live in the same geographic region. Scientists like Cynthia Moss have named these extended groupings "family groups" or "allied groups." Meetings between family groups are extremely joyous, as if they were close blood relations. The young are pleased to meet their playmates once again. They may remain near to one another for several weeks before separating but, all in all, they are often in contact. Various field studies have shown that this familiarity results from blood relations between some of the females in the groups. They are part of a clan that unites all the animals that may reproduce in a certain region.

The living space required by a clan is defined by natural or artificial limits and covers everything that its members may require, like grazing lands, water sources, saltpans, etc. The nature and intensity of greetings between elephants depends on the identities of the animals and the ties that bind them. For example, when two families that are not closely associated meet one another, the salutes are limited, and only the more extrovert young will prod the tip of their trunk into the mouth of another animal, while the adults pass one another in silence.

Here on the banks of the Ewase Ngiro, adolescents of both sexes play together, simulating fights, locking trunks, or simply resting against or rubbing one another.

The size of a herd is not constant, so it is difficult to give even an average number. Most often, the number varies between 3 and 15. In Amboseli, for example, of the 800 elephants registered, 160 are solitary bulls. The others are grouped in 50 families, each of about a dozen animals. Many researchers have worked on the size of herds in different regions of Africa and they have demonstrated that not only does the environment in which the elephants live—forest or savannah—influence this number, but the pressure exerted by poaching also does. As a result of hunting, the studies carried out 20 years ago or so are completely out of date both, owing both to the death of most of the elephants and to the recomposition of herds.

The degree of stability of a family depends on geographical conditions and the character of the elephants themselves, all of whom differ. The behavior of elephant families in Amboseli differs from that in Manyara or Zimbabwe owing to the ecology of each zone. In Amboseli, for example, families assemble in large herds when conditions permit. This phenomenon is accompanied by an increase in social exchanges, for instance, young males go in search of other young males in families they know less well to play and to test their strength. Adult females verify their position in the hierarchy by threatening, and sometimes chasing away, other females, and then re-establishing old contacts or creating new ones. Elephants seem to like these large herds.

The stability of families is threatened by the pressure exerted by poachers. They have understood the role of the matriarch and have generally concentrated their attacks on her. If she dies, her family becomes completely vulnerable and disorganized owing to the lack of leadership. When the matriarch is gone, the bonds between the females may loosen and the families break up. In the long term, poaching removes the elderly females which means that leadership is assumed by younger females with little experience. Another result is that the disorganization of the herds reduces the number of young elephants that reach maturity. It has been demonstrated that in certain regions of the savannah, where there is a high number of poachers, the surviving elephants group in large herds, at times over one hundred in number, as they no longer dare to move around in small groups. They think that by coming together they will offer each other greater protection against the poachers, or perhaps it is the young females who prefer to bring their groups together because they are inexpert in leading them. Various other factors will increase the instability in a family: its size (beyond a certain number food gets hard to find for everyone); the strength of the ties between certain individuals; and the presence of orphans. All these factors may combine but the commonest causes of the break up of a group are ecological: a strong or long drought can cause divisions even in the most stable of families. The merging of groups during the rainy season, when food is abundant, may be temporary—or they may become permanent.

THE LANGUAGE OF ELEPHANTS

92
Young elephants, no longer weaning, play as soon as they can, measuring their respective strength in harmless tussles.

93
Gluttons for dum palm fruit, elephants chase away the baboons already feeding on them.

Elephants communicate using a series of sounds and gestures. The commonest sounds are blares they produce through their trunks, which no one could forget after a stay in Africa. The sound is produced by air vibrated by the passage of sound waves created in the resonance box that is the trunk. Emitted from the larynx, the sounds are reinforced and modulated in the trunk, which the elephant is able to close partially or totally with the aid of two "lips." In addition, a thin fibrous septum that separates the two breathing ducts about 4-6 inches from the tip of the trunk reinforces this sound modulations. These blaring sounds are able to express all sorts of feelings and are used to accompany certain events. They can be like the sound of a trumpet used as an alarm, a muttering of joy used to greet other elephants, or a guttural sound that expresses sadness. They can also reflect fear or anger before a charge, while weak or mournful high-pitched blares indicate a feeling of isolation. In all, the range of audible sounds is very wide.

However, sound communication between elephants is not limited to these noises, but it was not until the 1980s that confirmation was given. Many observers had recognized that certain inexplicable phenomena were occurring, for example, they detected a sort of vibration emanating from elephants even though there was no sound; moreover, the animals would suddenly go stiff for no apparent reason. Furthermore, how could synchronized behavior between distant groups be explained? Kat Payne, a bioacoustics expert from Cornell University, made a very important discovery at the beginning of the 1980s when, having worked for twelve years on communication between whales, she began to study Asian elephants in

Portland Zoo in Oregon. She was able to confirm that they communicated using very low frequencies that lay outside the range of the human ear. In order to hear these sounds, it was necessary to record them on tape and replay them at ten times the normal speed. This experiment was corroborated by recordings made at Amboseli. The human ear can only perceive frequencies above 20 hertz, whereas elephants emit infrasounds at frequencies between 5 and 28 hertz, meaning that most of them are inaudible to us. Elephants were the first terrestrial mammals known to make use of this phenomenon. Later discoveries showed that hippopotami also use infrasound, and that elephants are unable to hear sounds at frequencies higher than 12,000 hertz. In comparison, bats can detect sounds as high as 80,000 hertz, dogs and monkeys as high as 40,000 hertz, but man only as high as 20,000 hertz.

In Amboseli, Dr. Joyce Poole, an American zoologist and researcher of elephants' communication systems, investigated Kate Payne's findings in greater depth. Dr. Poole was particularly interested in the content of the messages transmitted in this way and on their influence on the behavior of individuals; in her studies she succeeded in recording more than 25 different signals used in particular contexts. Infrasound travels over long distances and is less affected by obstacles than high frequencies. In normal conditions, elephants are able to communicate at distances up to 2.5 miles but certain infrasounds recorded at Amboseli also traveled 6 miles and could be as loud as 115 decibels. In the evening, the air temperature at a height of 975 feet begins to fall, and this causes low frequency sounds to be pulled downward toward the ground instead of allowing normal dispersion

94
This male is in musth – the highly active hormonal state – and his whole body is indicative of it.

95
When it charges, an elephant extends its ears to increase the impression of power.

96
The females have scented danger. The herd halts and its members lift their trunks to the wind.

97
Trunks have their own language. When an animal raises it, folded at the tip, it means perplexity or indecision.

of the sounds in the air. In other words, at dusk elephants are best able to communicate "silently" over longer distances. Nonetheless, Kate Payne's field research showed that elephants use this method of communication most often in the late afternoon.

The extraordinary potential of infrasound is recognized on seeing a herd's reaction to the reception of such a message: one moment all the members are eating, bathing or drinking peacefully, and the next they all raise their heads together. Such behavior means that they have either heard a danger signal or have smelled the hormonal messages of a female. Infrasound also explains how elephants are able to remain in contact to coordinate movements or group behavior at long distance; also how the slaughter of entire families in Zimbabwe is perceived by groups of elephants far away from the site; naturally, such an event upsets them greatly. Infrasound takes social communication to levels never suspected in the animal kingdom. Links between groups allow social relationships to remain strongly consolidated and are indispensable for preventing wastage of energy or time in keeping the group united on long journeys. Other tests have shown that elephants seem incapable of recognizing where the sounds come from, and are able to pass right by the source of the sounds without locating them. However, they are very capable of distinguishing between resonances, music, and sounds.

Different gestures and modes of behavior are another form of communication. The position of the trunk, for example, is very important. If the animal holds it up or sticks it out in front, then it is in a state of alertness. If the trunk is lifted but the tip is allowed to point downward, then the creature is perplexed or undecided. If the trunk is lowered and twisted from one side to the other, it is experiencing a conflict between fear and curiosity. In general, a charge with the trunk stuck forward is a bluff. When elephants meet, the trunk is used as a means of recognition or signaling a truce. It is also used to promote social cohesion between members of the same family group.

Ears too are used as a means of expression, both by their position and by the sounds they can make. When it holds it ears open, half closed or flat against its neck, the elephant is transmitting a state of excitement or worry. When a threat is detected or if an elephant wishes to intimidate an adversary, it opens its ears wide at the side of its head, tripling the width of the frontal view. When grazing or resting (and when not flapping its ears to promote coolness, the elephant holds them folded back or just slightly open; when it is feeling curious, it half or fully opens them. When frightened, an elephant it will take very characteristic diagonal steps, pull its head down into its shoulders, and hold its ears flat. The flapping sounds of the ears are of different types; they range from attempted intimidation to signals that either call other elephants or suggest departure.

Elephants express their sentiments in their own manner. The joy they feel after the birth of a calf, during playtime, or when meeting a friend or a member of the family (or even a human friend) is very evident. Secretions from the temporal glands are also part of the communication system they use, and these represent a state of excitement or restlessness. The secretions are most obvious when elephants greet one another or when young males fight, but are also present when an animal is isolated from his family. Females secrete this hormonal liquid throughout the year but the phenomenon is most frequent during the dry season. The liquid of each elephant probably has an individual odor that other elephants, with their highly developed sense of smell, are able to recognize.

All descriptions of the social life of elephants paint a picture of uniform behavior, at least in a given region, but each animal has its own character and reactions differ between individuals. Elephants do not have stereotyped behavior: even if you have been told that an elephant's first charge is always purely for intimidatory reasons, you are advised not to test the theory!

98 top
Physical contact is important in elephants'
social life; they often touch one another with
their trunks, or rest against and stroke one
another.

98 bottom
In many species play is only for the young. In
the case of elephants, however, even the adult
females play when the conditions are right.

99
Contrary to appearance, these females are only
playing, an activity they often indulge in.

100-101
When two herds meet, the greetings between
the females may develop into locked trunks or
'nose to nose' encounters.

102
The dense vegetation in Samburu can hide a female; this one has unexpectedly begun to charge.

103
With ears fully extended and trunk lifted in a fearsome blare, a charging elephant makes a terrifying impression.

104
An adolescent is straggling behind the herd which, farther down, is bathing quietly. The animal is alarmed by the arrival of an adult male.

105
The authors were violently charged by the matriarch of a herd in Tsavo Park. Starting from a large distance away, she launched herself at their vehicle without warning. Later they discovered that, some time before, poachers had been at work in the same area.

106-107
*This matriarch has launched herself in a simple
intimidatory charge. However arresting, such
behavior is not dangerous.*

108-109
*As nature has decreed, this thirtysomething male
lives alone in a territory that he only leaves when
he is in musth–in search of females.*

110
*Males yonger than thirty or so
live in groups of 2 to 30
individuals.*

111
*These two adult males occupy
the same hierarchical rank.
Neither of the two will give
way, with the result that a
battle for a female in heat is
inevitable.*

THE SOCIAL LIFE OF MALE ELEPHANTS

There are no points of contact between the life of adult males and that enjoyed by the families of elephants. Males offer each other little or no support or companionship. The strong emotional ties between the females are absent, nor is it possible to compare their social structure with that of baboons where, for example, the large males ensure collective security. When they become mature, young males see their life change. Having been long spoilt by the matriarchal group, they begin to experience increasing rejection from by the females in their family when they reach maturity–until they recognize that they are no longer wanted. However, this behavior does not seem to be produced systematically. Some observers have seen young males chased away by adult males or by other males who have left to live separately of their own choosing. The ties between the young male, who leaves his family, and his mother loosen but are not broken immediately. In the first period of separation, the family keeps an eye on the young male but, little by little, the distance grows. Fights with other males of similar age and weight continue, and these young bulls go in search of other males to form a band of celibate males of approximately the same size and age (roughly from 10 to 17) after which they have reached adulthood.

In physical terms, these groups remain relatively close to their families but later, once they have become adults, the males form groups that offer greater cohesion between individuals, even if their structure remains more open than that of the family groups. These male groups can number from as few as 3 to up to 30 males, but once they have reached the age of 30, the males turn solitary. Far from the females, they inhabit well-defined territories which they do not leave except to search for females to mate with. Sexually mature males are only tolerated within the families when one of the females is in heat. The famous Ngorongoro crater in Tanzania is a site that well exemplifies the division of space between elephants on a sexual basis. In this reserve, the old males spend most of their time at the bottom of the crater while the families–the females and young–inhabit the forests that cover the slopes of the ancient volcano. The males of intermediate age wander between the two.

Not all males over 30 live alone. Some prefer to live with a couple of companions a little younger than themselves, rather as though it were a men's club. Outside of the period of sexual activity (musth), the males feed, rest, wallow in mud and cover themselves with dust far from the females and young. It is a period of tranquility during which the males put on weight and store reserves of energy. All large males form routines based on a settled lifestyle, and in Samburu some were so fixed in their habits that we met them on the same path at the same time for several mornings in a row.

Although they live without any apparent social structure, the males have their own hierarchy that begins to be formed from their early youth. All those

112-113
Only males live on the bottom
of Ngorongoro Crater; the
females and young live higher
up the slopes or on the
summit. This is a clear
illustration of the division of
space between the sexes.

belonging to the same clan come to know each other over the years. The games are quickly dropped and each one has his own identity that allows him to establish his role in the group and determine his position with regard to feeding, drinking or mating.

As the young male grows, the challenges that he issues to other males, or to which he responds, become increasingly serious but never degenerate into real combat. When two males fight, it is really a friendly tussle during which they each test their own strength. The two approach one another, touch the tip of the other's trunk and, at times, also the temporal glands. Then they hold one another's trunk, and place their own on the head of the adversary. Tusks set against tusks, they begin to push, then back off a little before throwing themselves at each other. When you hear the crack of ivory against ivory, it seems impossible that these games do not cause greater damage. In particular, in games of this sort the eyes of the opponent are never attacked.

By the time they reach adulthood, the males in a clan have generally all met one another, whether as infants or in the groups of adolescents. The outcomes of all the games has remained in the collective memory so that, when two male adults meet, their already know their respective social status. The less strong gives way to the dominant without a challenge having to be issued, so that rivalry is resolved by simple rituals.

114 and 115
*These three adolescent males have not yet left
their birth herd but will soon have to. The
afternoon this photograph was taken, these
three played for over 90 minutes.*

116 and 117
*Once the playfulness of adolescence has passed,
the time of combat between elephants of the
same age – or older individuals – arrives. Long,
hard fights establish a hierarchy between
individuals but never end with the death of the
weaker of the two.*

ELEPHANTS AND DEATH

A young female slows up behind the herd. Her mother is walking ahead with a baby elephant just a few months old. Suddenly, the young female lets out a piteous trumpet before sinking to her knees and lying down on the ground. Worried, the mother heads back with her youngest and other companions. The rest of the herd halt and watch without intervening. The mother approaches her daughter, offers her trunk to reassure the young female and to spur her to stand up, but in vain. She then slips one of her feet beneath the youngster's back and pushes, helping her at the same time with her trunk. She tries this maneuver several times, both with her front feet and her tusks. For a moment she succeeds in getting the calf into a seated position but, inert, the body falls back to the ground. Thick secretions flow down the temples of the mother and daughter, and of other members of the herd.

Within an hour, the young female dies. Swept up by a sort of frenzy, a number of females kneel to try to lift her. Others try other methods to bring her back: they strike her with their feet or tusks, and one even goes to fetch some grass and poke it into the youngster's mouth. In the end, the herd recognizes that there is nothing that can be done. For a long time the mother sniffs her daughter, then all the members of the herd surround the body and touch it with their trunks to absorb some of its odor. Hours pass. The youngest are attached, unmoving, to their mothers as though they understood the gravity of the situation. Eventually, the eldest females set off again

but, after just a short distance, they turn to the dead body, straighten their trunks and trumpet. The mother, completely confused and lost, follows the herd, then makes a half turn. She continues this uncertain behavior several times but, in the end, joins the rest of the herd that waits for her a little farther away.

There have been very many descriptions of the reaction of elephants to the death of a relative, and they are all similar. Cynthia Moss described that, on the death of a matriarch, her family used their feet and trunks to gather some earth and stones and spread it over her body, then some of the females went to gather branches from the nearby bushes and placed them on top. By the end of the day, the matriarch had been almost completely buried with earth and branches. For much of the night, the herd kept a vigil over her body and it was only shortly before dawn that they reluctantly left the site.

Derek and Beverly Joubert, photographers for National Geographic, also recounted strange ceremonies: the old bull elephant in Botswana referred to as M40 was about to die. The other males came in groups of two or three to sniff every inch of his body in a ritual that was especially moving for the silence in which it was performed. As M40 was dying, and shortly after his death, the young males approached and mounted him as if they were trying to mate with him, in an act that may be linked to the concept of hierarchy. When an elephant passes near a place where

118 and 119
A male has broken the back of
a young female with whom he
was trying to mate. He will
remain with her until she dies,
but will then leave her body to
the hyenas and vultures.

a relation has died, it remains immobile and silent for several minutes, even years after the death.

It is also surprising to see how elephants recognize the corpses and skeletons of their relations while they completely ignore those of other species. They always react when confronted by the body of a dead elephant; they back up a few paces and stand silent and tense. Then, they extend their trunks toward the remains of the animal to smell it and then approach gently and carefully. They touch the bones, sometimes lifting them and moving them, paying, it seems, particular interest to the head and tusks.

Even a pile of bare, bleached bones will halt a group of elephants that comes across it for the first time. They push the bones around and sometimes carry them elsewhere. Once, Cynthia Moss took back to her camp the jaw of an adult female to determine the elephant's exact age at death. Some weeks later, the family of the dead female was passing near the camp and made a deviation to examine the jaw. A young male, 7 years of age, stayed long after the rest of the family had moved on. He touched it and turned it with his feet and trunk. Had he realized that this was the remains of his mother?

It is clear that elephants have a notion of death and, to us, this is their strangest and most disconcerting characteristic. It is possible to talk of a respect for death, and this goes to show how strong the bonds are among the members of a family.

We tend to think we are the only living creatures able to think in a complex manner and to feel the entire range of emotions. However, many field observations illustrate the depth of emotions experienced by elephants. One of the most natural—most human—is the sadness felt at the death of a near one. Watching the expression on the face and the behavior of a female crying over the death of a newborn calf, one gets the impression that every part of her is expressing sorrow: her eyes and mouth, and the way she holds her ears, her head and body. Joyce Poole also described the sight of a mother attempting to bring her dead baby back to life. Human beings express the same denial of reality when faced by the death of a dear one.

Dr. Poole was able to observe the extent of the sadness felt by a group of elephants on another occasion. A herd of females was moving towards new territory when, suddenly, one of them fell. When her companions returned to her side, they understood immediately the gravity of the situation. They tried to raise her but without success. Eventually, the males who were accompanying the group attempted to mate with her, clearly hoping to bring her back to a state of consciousness. As she did not react, in the end the elephants left the body and continued their march but, the next day, they returned to "mourn" and pay tribute to their dead companion. It seems that elephants have a need to remember and to mourn their dead loved ones.

MATING

120 left
The difference in size and weight between the male and female is very marked, with an average disparity of one and a half tons.

120 right
There is no defined mating season but sexual activity is more intense during the rainy season.

122
In the presence of a calf, a male touches the genital organs of a female and sniffs her urine to ascertain if she is in heat.

123
If the first female is not willing, the male will examine the others in turn.

We are in our favorite spot in Amboseli, near "Observation Hill," watching the small herd we usually follow. A large solitary bull is moving toward us with his head held high. The musth glands behind his eyes are overflowing with a thick liquid and urine is dripping from the greenish sheath of his penis, indicating sexual readiness. His is still a hundred yards or so away, but already the females are raising their trunks and trumpeting. They all watch him arrive with suspicion. As he approaches, we start the engine so we are ready to leave quickly if he turns aggressive, which is not uncommon among males in musth. We remember the day a male followed us into the marsh to within a few yards of the vehicle. We reverse a thousand yards or so but still without feeling completely safe.

The smell of the male is bitter and strong. When he is just a short distance from the females, he slows and lowers his head, wrapping his trunk around one of his tusks. The females relax and begin to give out little blares of excitement. The male approaches one of the females and places the tip of his trunk on her vulva. Another female begins to urinate and he goes over, places the tip of his trunk in the urine and then in his mouth. He stays still for a moment, then restarts his inspection of all the females in the group. In the end he walks off without having found what he was looking for. In all, he stayed with the herd for about twenty minutes.

A week passes. One morning, we find a young female from the herd, whom we had named Lucie, near the hill. She was running across the plain, trying to escape the attentions of a young male. Her family was not nearby, so she must have wandered away when the male was following her. For more than an hour the pair continue their chase, occasionally stopping to get their breath back. Finally, the male gets close enough to rest his trunk on her back. Lucie stops still and he attempts to mount her, but he does not succeed properly and ejaculates outside her vulva. The two begin to graze but shortly after the chase restarts, and we continue to follow the spectacle. The male makes several attempts and finally succeeds in his aim, and Lucie rejoins her family in the marsh, followed by her admirer. Other males, attracted by the state of the young female, begin to circle the herd. Lucie hardly has time to eat before the males are once more hounding her.

When we rejoin the herd the next day, the whole business begins again. In the afternoon, the entire herd leaves the marsh and, at that moment, we see the bull we had seen the week before. The females get excited at his approach; they turn, back away, extend their ears, urinate and stick their trunks out toward him, trumpeting. Even the young males approach to sniff but the other males who were following Lucie retired to a safe distance when they became aware of the large bull. They all eat, watching him out of the corner of their eye. When the bull approaches the young female, she begins to run, but in a less convincing manner than before. Quickly, he arrives and places his trunk on her back, and she stops still. She gives off a shrill blare and all her family members hurry over to her and surround the pair. Lucie offers herself to the male, holding onto his rump and backing away. The male mounts her, keeping his hind

124
From 12 years of age, males are theoretically sexually mature but generally have to wait several years before being accepted as older animals have priority.

125
A female, clearly recognizable by her diminutive size, wanders away from her family with a male with whom, after an hour of courtship, she will mate.

feet on the ground. The copulation lasts about thirty seconds and the entire family blast out a cacophony of trumpeting. All the animals are very excited and the spectacle is very impressive. When it is over, Lucie stands by her bull while the females come to sniff her vulva. As we leave, Lucie is grazing beside the large bull; the other males no longer come over because they know they have no chance of getting near Lucie.

The next day, nothing has changed. Lucie and the bull mate twice more. Then the day after, he begins to lose interest in her and heads off during the morning. Lacking his protection, Lucie is once more assailed by the young males. Fortunately she is going off heat and, when that occurs, life returns to its normal tranquility. The males, however, do not distance themselves from the family because Lucie's aunt is now in heat. However, having so much more experience, she does not allow herself to be importuned by the young males.

Not all couplings go so well. Recently, in the Masai-Mara, a powerful male wanted to couple with a very young female but, when he mounted her, he split her kidneys. Watched over by the male, who was very aggressive toward other elephants, the female died. He did not abandon her until the vultures and hyenas came to take possession of her corpse.

Adult males, particularly when they are over 30 years of age, enter a very marked sexual condition known as musth. The condition, like an uncontrollable fever, results in excessive secretions from the temporal glands, which swell and exude a thick, bitter liquid which can be smelt at a distance, even by humans. During this period, the males rub their heads against trees to mark them with their odor and also seem to suffer from incontinence, as

the insides of their hind thighs are continually bathed with urine. The penis takes on a strange greenish color and the sheath is covered with a sort of foam.

The word musth comes from Hindi and refers to the physiological and psychological state that periodically affects mature male elephants. The phenomenon has long been known in Asia because it renders the animals dangerous, especially tame elephants, for the 2 or 3 months that it lasts. Musth is not linked to a particular season, and the males enter the condition at different times. In healthy males, the condition repeats itself at the same time each year.

In Africa, this state passed unobserved for a long time. Experts knew about the musth of male Asiatic elephants, in which secretions from the temporal glands were considered one of the main signs of the beginning of the condition. However, in Africa the females and young have the same secretions throughout the year and it was deduced that in African elephants these secretions must have a different significance. It was only in the 1980s that biologists began to get interested in musth in Africa, in particular with the studies Dr. Joyce Poole undertook in Amboseli.

When a male enters musth, his behavior and personality alter. He becomes bad tempered and turns his aggressiveness on his companions and any outside elements, like tourist vehicles or researchers who have come to study him. There is an increase in testosterone, the male hormone, in his blood and his general behavior changes to such an extent that Joyce Poole claims she can recognize a male in musth from a distance just by his gait. He holds his head high, his chin in and advances with long, determined steps.

The condition is accompanied by particular behavior and postures: males in musth have a special manner of moving their ears quite unlike that of males not in the same state, and it is possible that these movements are used to waft the smell of their glandular secretion forward. There are also curious movements of the trunk, which is often held up to their forehead.

The principal consequence of musth is the upsetting of the hierarchical order in the male population. This hierarchy is partly based on size—and therefore age—and every male knows his position. The dominant male imposes his rights over the others, for example, by having the best branch of a tree that has been knocked down. But when a male is in musth, this order is upset and he takes precedence over all the others, even those of higher station, and refuses to put up with any obligation. He will happily challenge those who are in theory stronger than him. He leaves the customary territory to go in search of females. In a state of nervousness, he runs from one group to another. When he finds one to his liking, i.e., one that is receptive, he goes crazy. He hardly has time to feed or rest as he is obliged to chase off other males and protect the female. He wants to be sure that he is the father of the future offspring. He will even challenge another male in musth who has come to the female with the same purpose. As a consequence of this behavior, in particular owing to running great distances, he loses weight rapidly, and this continues throughout the period of musth. Fortunately, this extravagant behavior does not last all year! When the condition comes to an end, the male returns to his habitual place and physical and psychological state.

Researchers have observed that musth often begins around 30 years of age and believe that it probably plays a fundamental role in the selection of parents. Males reach sexual maturity around 12 and from this age are able to mate and procreate but, under normal conditions, this is a rare occurrence. Neither the females nor older males allow young males to couple with females. Generally, males begin to compete for the attention of fertile females at around age 25 but can hope to be successful only when no older males are around. Males between 36 and 50, in theory, have better chances, with precedence given to those in musth. It appears that a male does not enter musth if other, hierarchically superior, males who live in the same zone are already in musth. This occurs to minimize conflict. However, a male able to mate will cede his place to another male in musth, and this second male will then protect the fertile female during the crucial period of ovulation. In short, it is usual that the fathers of all the young elephants in a certain population will be older than 30 years.

When a male in musth smells the trace of an older male also in musth, he sniffs around and looks around anxiously, trying to locate his rival. It is also possible that he will reduce his quantities of urine and glandular secretions in order not to face a rival who is too dangerous for him. On the other hand, when two males of similar standing are in musth, one may look for the other to challenge him. During fights between two males in musth, the rituals of hierarchy are ignored. The combatants advance, heads high, ears extended, and without

The arrival of an adult male next to a female in heat immediately results in the giving way of the younger males.

the preliminary exploration of each other with their trunks. They immediately begin sideways movements so that they do not allow the other an opening from the side, then, they throw themselves against each other in short, rapid and precise charges with all their strength, attempting to thrust their tusks into the most vulnerable parts of their adversary's body. Sometimes they attempt to throw the other off balance by locking tusks and pushing. When one of the two males falls to the ground, his rival may pierce his head or flank with his tusk and kill him. Some battles can last 8 hours or more.

Do males of over 30 still exist? Sadly, having the longest and strongest tusks, few of this age survive poachers. In consequence, the role of musth in the reproduction of African elephants is far less important than it used to be.

At times, an inexpert eye will have difficulty telling the sex of an elephant as their sexual organs are very different to those of other mammals. The vulva is situated in the lower part of the abdomen, as in Sirenids and other marine mammals, and even male elephants often have difficulty in finding it. As for the males, the testicles are permanently located inside the abdomen.

Females reach sexual maturity around 8 years of age, which is when they start to be in heat 4 times a year for a period of 3 to 6 days each time. Their behavior when in heat is as follows: on the first day, sometimes the first two, the female will evade the approaches of males. During this phase she moves with a gait that is referred to as estral, with her ears held straight out, her head high and slightly on one

side; this is the phase during which the males follow her. During her observations of female elephants in heat, Cynthia Moss has noticed that a sufficiently expert female can usually keep attendant males at bay. She is not obliged to mate with them all indiscriminately, but when copulation does occur, the female and her family indulge in noisy accompaniment. This agitation attracts other males, which is unquestionably the purpose.

During the second phase of the period of heat, the female is joined by a large male with whom she mates willingly and by whom she lets herself be protected. Studies in Amboseli have shown that 87% of these males are in musth. The pair may remain together for anything between 2 hours and 3 days, and it is a quiet period in that the female will not be bothered by other males. The third phase begins with the large male taking his leave, whereupon the young males restart their siege of the female.

In the case of inexpert females, either ovulating for the first time or who are barely into their sexual maturity, these phases do not apply. The females are followed and besieged while in heat and males of all ages mount them repeatedly. It seems, therefore, that pair behavior is acquired.

Females can be in heat at any moment in the year, though in certain regions peaks have been noted, for example, in the middle of the rainy season, which causes a rash of births at the start of the rainy season two years later. As the male weighs up to twice as much as the female, mating never lasts more than 45 seconds and the male carries his weight on his hind legs, with his front legs resting

127

An elephant's penis can be almost 4 feet long and 4 inches in diameter. It is highly mobile and perfectly adapted to the genital organs of the female.

on the female's back. His penis is very flexible, almost 4 feet long and 4 inches in diameter. The male is obliged to wait on average 8 hours between copulations.

In practice, during her adult life, the female is only sexually receptive for a few days every four years as ovulation does not restart on average for two years following the birth of a calf. This interval of four years (a 2-year pregnancy and a 2-year wait) may be reduced if the calf dies young. How do large bull elephants in musth find the females when they are receptive if their in-heat period is so brief? Long-distance communication is of great use to elephants at this time. After mating, even with a young male, the female and her family blast out powerful trumpeting sounds comprising infrasonic components which travel over long distances. These attract other males to the female in heat, particularly males in musth. They too emit very low, powerful sounds that attract receptive females while repelling males of a lower hierarchic status.

The members of a single group are, by definition, linked by blood. The phenomenon of musth reduces the sexual activity of the males to just a few months a year and, in doing so, ensures that there is little likelihood that the same mother will give birth to consecutive calves fathered by the same male. Yet the young in a family, born at intervals of a few months, will probably be the offspring of the same male. In addition, the females in a family tend to come into heat at intervals of a few weeks from one another. When a dominant male in musth finds himself in the neighborhood of a female in heat, he will probably become the father of all the young conceived during that period. Going into heat may also result from the musth of a particular male, and, as such, would be partly a choice on the part of the female.

The newborn calves in a family will therefore be the half-brothers and -sisters of their fellow offspring on their father's side. On their mother's side, they will be the half-brothers and -sisters of some of the elder young, and become the aunts and uncles of younger members of the family in the years to come.

Unfavorable environmental conditions, such as drought, prevent ovulation in adult females. During the 1970s, following three years of reduced rainfall and two years of drought in Amboseli, Cynthia Moss noted a heavy drop in births of elephants: in 1974 29% of the adult females gave birth; in 1975, only 8%; and in 1976 none. At the same time, the females going into heat for the first time were late, and had to wait until they were 14 or 15 years of age, and in other regions they had to wait until they were about 20. Consequently, unfavorable circumstances can delay the age of puberty and increase the average period between births from 4 years to almost 8 years.

The effects of such circumstances are quickly felt in a population, as females only give birth to one calf at a time. When the density of elephants in a region becomes too high, there is a regulation of the number of births, but, during heavy rainy seasons, sexual activity spurts and males of all ages unite in large groups that form where the vegetation is abundant.

128
Very often the family of the female in heat stands around the mating pair. Then they all emit powerful blares that travel long distances owing to their infrasonic properties.

129
This female is secreting copiously from her temporal glands. All elephants, regardless of sex or age, produce the same secretions when they are excited. The hormonal liquid of the young and the females is not so thick or strong smelling as that of males in musth.

130-131
A young male watches his mother as she mates. On average ovulation restarts two years after a birth but it can be inhibited if conditions are not favorable, for example, during periods of drought.

THE YOUNG

132 left
A young elephant tests the food
of his companion with his
trunk.

132 right
Tusks begin to appear on young
elephants from two years of age.

134 and 135
An elephant's pregnancy lasts
22 months. Newly born calves –
minuscule in comparison to their
mothers even though they weigh
more than 220 pounds – are
covered with dark hair.

136
Clumsy but stubborn, a baby tries
to master the use of his trunk.

137
Babies are suckled for a couple of
years, but from 6 months their diet
is integrated with plants and grass.

THE YOUNG

The whole family is gathered around Chloe, who is about to give birth. As the calf is born, the family trumpets and blares and the hormonal secretions from their temporal glands run down their cheeks. Chloe has had at least two offspring and knows what she is doing. She frees the newborn elephant from the placenta with her tusks and the surrounding females point their trunks toward the mother and son. Chloe prompts the baby elephant to stand up but he falls down immediately. She helps him by gently placing a foot beneath his stomach and supporting him with her trunk. On the fourth attempt, he finally succeeds in standing on his own feet. He stretches his trunk constantly in the direction of his mother. The young females gather closely round him and caress him with their trunks. With two hours or so of his birth, the baby elephant is able to take his first steps. A half hour more and he succeeds in reaching Chloe's udder. He sucks vigorously for a few minutes as his mother grazes. An hour later and he is walking behind Chloe, though not very quickly. Nightfall obliges us to leave the scene, but we rejoin the group a few days later where they are grazing on nutritious land in the company of other families. Many elephants have been born in the last few months.

Chloe's son is unable to climb over a tree trunk in his path. Immediately, Chloe and two other females attend to him. Trumpeting, they help him to overcome the obstacle by placing their trunks beneath his belly and practically lifting him off the ground. The baby shakes his head and gives off a curious cry. The females respond with gentle hoots and touch him with their trunks to reassure him. All around the families pasture peacefully enjoying the ubiquitous fodder. The youngest take the chance to play while the young males gather to indulge in exuberant behavior. A young female watches them for a moment, then picks up a piece of wood with her trunk and tosses it in the air. Another female prefers to play with clumps of earth, throwing them up onto her back. The small calves imitate their elders and follow them, climbing on one another and running in all directions for no apparent reason. Only the babies remain close to their mothers, but when we try to observe them, they hide behind the bulk of their relatives. The others cry, yell and trumpet without the adults paying any attention. At a sign from the matriarch, the females move off and, finding themselves suddenly alone, the youngsters halt the game and chase after the herd. They run in a relaxed manner, shaking their heads from side to side, flapping their ears against their necks and letting out powerful blares from their trunks. Having arrived at a place where the vegetation is thick, they begin to stamp on the bushes and push through with their heads and tusks. A young adult joins them, and the sound of trumpeting rends the air. Then calm returns. The herd breaks up once again and the families disperse to browse the grass. A flash of lightning is followed by a rumble of thunder, and a very young male cries in fear. His elder sister reassures him by placing her trunk in his mouth.

Chloe's family had gradually approached us but now they are keeping their distance. One of the younger ones comes to look at us from a closer vantage point. His mother and aunt demonstrate their worry by lifting first one foot, then another. Another small male joins the first, then raises his trunk and tries a little charge, trying to intimidate us. At the same time he trumpets loudly as a sign of alert. The females come after him and look at us a little threateningly so we decide to back off a little. The young male trembles with emotion, he had allowed himself to get scared by nothing. Then everything calms down again and the herd approaches us as if nothing had happened.

A young male of about 4 years doesn't seem to appreciate that his mother is feeding his baby sister. He is envious and would like to suck at the teat too, so he follows his mother closely, wraps his trunk around her rear leg and rubs himself against her, but she refuses to give way to him. He responds with a sort of upset wail. It's not always easy being a youngster.

138
Mothers hold a foreleg a little to one side to
allow their young to reach their teats.

139
Young calves are small enough to fit neatly
beneath their mothers' chests. This provides
then with shade from the sun and prevents
heatstroke.

A baby often seeks physical contact with its
mother, touching her with its trunk or other
parts of its body.

141
Resting against the trunk of its mother, who
wishes to eat some grass, this youngster is trying
to imitate her by grabbing the stalks with its trunk.

THE EDUCATION OF THE YOUNG

142
After three or four months, a baby elephant is able to use its trunk to eat.

143
Baby elephants drink up to 3 gallons of milk a day. They drink with their mouths, holding their trunks over their heads.

Even for seasoned elephant watchers, it is rare to observe a birth. Most occur at night or, if during the day, in sheltered areas hidden from the gaze of others. Birth takes place after a 22-month pregnancy, and is often surrounded by females of the family. When the future mother is experienced, generally everything happens without problems. At birth, the baby elephant weighs about 220 pounds, stands 33 inches tall at the shoulder and is covered in black hair. During the first few minutes, the mother pushes the baby to stand him up as he needs her milk fairly soon: it is a question of survival. As a rule, the baby takes his first steps after an hour or so, then quickly finds his mother's teats slightly behind her front legs. From the moment he begins to drink his mother's milk, the baby gains in strength, so that several hours after his birth, he is able to follow the herd. A female without experience, however, does not always know what to do. Cynthia Moss once witnessed a very young mother leave her newborn baby in the full sunshine for three hours without suckling him. She was unable to help him find her nipples and lost her head.

During the first hours and days of life, the baby is disoriented. He can hardly see and he recognizes his mother only by smell, by the sounds she makes, and by touch. He can walk, but not stably, and needs to be freed from all the roots and obstacles in his path. His trunk is his principal means of contact with the world, thanks to which he rapidly explores the environment around him. He uses it all the time to smell and touch

things. The other members of his family, usually the females, touch him with their long trunks, while the young males do not pay him much attention.

Elephants suckle using their mouth, raising their trunk over their head. To help their babies, mothers hold a front leg a little to the side, otherwise he cannot reach her udder, from which he drinks about 3 gallons of milk a day. He also enjoys going to the udders of the other females in the group who help to look after him, but they are too young to have any milk to offer. He will be suckled for two or three years, but from the age of 6 months his nourishment is complemented by fodder.

Newborn calves are not the only ones who want to be suckled; their siblings also want their turn. At times the mother will allow them to suck but more often than not she will refuse. The young males attempt to drink more frequently than the females and their growth is more rapid. Observers have remarked that the interval between two births is longer if the first baby is a male, therefore males are suckled for a longer period than females. This means that raising a young male demands more care and energy from the mother, but then, if his needs are not satisfied, he will die more quickly than a young female.

During the first few months, a youngster does not stray far from his mother's side and will often hide between her legs. He must also be protected from the sun's rays as his skin is tender. If he wanders off, his mother or a babysitter quickly follow him. He will frequently rest during the day, stretching out on the ground protected by the adults. The very young often

144-145
*Very young elephants
frequently place their trunks in
their mouths, rather like
children who suck their
thumbs for comfort.*

146 and 147
*Young elephants often play
with bits of wood and tufts of
grass, which gives them
practice in the use of their
trunks.*

let out little cries when they feel lost, though usually they have no real reason to do so. In the case of a baby, the mother will run to his side, but if he is slightly older, she allows the adolescents to help him, who sometimes form a crush around him. Females reassure youngsters by maternally placing the tip of their trunk in the baby's mouth. Females who are too young to have offspring take care of their younger brothers and sisters or their cousins, thereby learning some of the duties of motherhood.

The herd of females into which a calf is born is the depositary of the species' knowledge that is crucial to the calf's survival. Up to the age of 5, calves depend entirely on their mother and the other members of the family, and the level of care lavished on them is remarkable. Youngsters are touched, sniffed and caressed unceasingly. They are the objects of the attention from the whole group.

Babies are born with a minimum of innate knowledge or understanding. They learn by imitating and remembering their elders' behavior. Despite their precocious nature, young elephants do not know how to use their trunk correctly. As they grow, they learn what it can do, just like a human baby learns what its hands can do. With time, the trunk develops into the equivalent of a hand to pick up objects, scratch, drink, etc. First, they try to manipulate objects with their trunk, to pick up pieces of grass, and lift bits of bark or branches. Their clumsiness is comic when they try desperately, but in vain, to wrap their rubbery appendage round a piece of wood. They are unable command the multitude of muscles that control this complex organ, and, in fact, it can at times be a bothersome thing, swinging about in all directions. They will shake it vigorously and swing it in circles without really knowing what it is for, and they even trip over it!

The trunk can be used to provide comfort, and a baby may suck on its tip like a human baby sucks a thumb. By the time calves are 3 or 4 months old, they are generally dexterous enough to suck water up in their trunks and squirt it into their mouths, rather than get down on their bellies and drink directly. At the start, the water goes everywhere but within a month or so they will have acquired a certain ability. And around the age of 3 months they begin to eat grass that they often take from the mouths of elder siblings or to gather the plants that their mothers have dropped on the ground. A good way to learn which plants are edible is to acquire a personal taste! From the age of 6 months, an elephant can store away a hefty quantity of fodder each day.

Fewer than 1% of elephants are born as twins and, generally, they do not survive. Cynthia Moss once followed the growth of twins that managed to survive into adulthood. Each of the two sucked from one of their mother's two teats. The male was more aggressive and would push his sister so she would leave the nipple. To begin with, he usually managed to prevent her from sucking but then the female learned how to solve the problem. As the two played together a lot, the young female began to profit from her brother's tiredness to go and drink her mother's milk. After a few weeks, the shows of aggressiveness ceased.

The mother was a matriarch of great experience and one of the females most suited to raise the two. When they were born, there was plenty of vegetation and the mother seemed to produce enough milk for the two youngsters, so their survival was due to a fortunate combination of circumstances.

Baby elephants have a happy infancy. They are spoilt and are free from any responsibilities up to the age of 4. Around that time they have to learn the social life of the herd and its rules, but that does not prevent the young, especially the males, from having stern discipline imposed on them, right from an early age. For example, a young elephant who pushes his way forward to a river bank to ensure he can drink quickly may be knocked to the ground by a trunk, foot or shoulder to teach him his place.

Puberty begins between the 10th and 12th year; the young females soon become full members of the society of females of reproductive age and the males leave their group, more or less reluctantly. Some may leave as early as 9 years of age, whereas others remain until they are 15 or so.

148

Generally the father of births in a particular herd is a single male adult. Here, the baby with the back of his ears still a strong pink is only a few weeks old.

149

A mother and baby leave a marsh. Given her size, the water only came halfway up the mother but the youngster, quite clearly, had to get completely wet and swim to follow her.

150

Early morning: a young female plays with her younger brother. The rainy season has just finished so there is plenty of food available.

151

With a friend at his side, a mother encourages a baby elephant to cross a ditch by pushing him with her trunk.

152
*This inexpert youngster was unable to climb
back up onto the path. Hearing his cry, the
mother and another female raise him by putting
their trunks beneath his stomach.*

153
*The young rested while the females grazed. Now
the matriarch has given the signal to depart and
they have to get up.*

154
*A mother and her calf, accompanied by the inevitable
cattle egrets, advance down a path in Amboseli.*

154-155
*Seemingly unworried by the clouds of insects, a female
grazes, followed by her youngster.*

156 and 157
*Baby elephants are curious creatures: every noise,
every new animal attracts their attention and prompts
them to play.*

158-159
*The baby in the foreground prepares to cross a
path in the savannah in East Tsavo. Prompted
by maternal instinct, his mother hurries up to
protect him – or maybe to tell him off.*

PLAY

160-161
The make-believe combat between two youngsters seems to have finished with one of them yielding. The games between the young are never violent, and even those between adults are generally harmless.

162 and 163
Young elephants usually play with their contemporaries but are also happy to play with those more elderly. The trunk is a fundamental tool: using it, youngsters can push their mother, join themselves to the tail of a young female, or lock onto the trunk of an adult and play with it at will.

Elephants are one of the rare herbivore species in which the young spend much of their time playing when they are not feeding or sleeping. They play in a variety of ways: usually they indulge in head-to-head trials of strength; they chase one another, the chaser attacking the tail of his prey; and they love to climb on top of one another, especially during mud baths. In a really wet mud pool, there will be a pile of small elephants slipping, rolling, wriggling and wrapping themselves around one another. They take pleasure in the slightest thing – blades of grass, a branch or a leaf swaying in the wind. They are very curious creatures and are interested in all the creatures they see, whether they fly, climb, walk or swim. When a vehicle approaches them, the youngsters pretend to charge it, then, proudly, or perhaps frightened by their daring, they will return to hide behind their mother. From the age of 3 or 4, the young males mime the mating act.

When the dry season begins, the young elephants play loses its intensity and may cease altogether if this period is prolonged or if living conditions become difficult. But then, as soon as the grass turns green once more, the games restart and even the adults take part with enthusiasm.

The first manifestations of combat between young males are simply infantile games, often broken up by the females. As they grow, young males spend more and more time in ritual challenges, and the difference in lifestyles of the two sexes increases with the arrival of adolescence.

164
When they are not feeding or sleeping, the youngest elephants spend most of their time playing.

165
Games are more intense when there is plenty of food; during periods of drought, they may cease altogether.

166 and 167 top
After resting under the protection of the adults, two babies begin to play.

167 bottom
Two youngsters test their strength in a simulated tussle.

FEEDING

168 left
Elephants are choosy eaters: they prefer the tenderest leaves and use their trunks to strip them from a tree's highest branches.

168 right
An adult elephant can feed for up to 18 hours a day.

170
By tearing off the bark, this female has condemned an acacia to death. In the past, when elephants migrated at will, such behavior was less damaging; vegetation had time to grow back. Within parks and reserves, there is now far less opportunity for regrowth.

171
Elephants eat huge quantities of grass and practically all species of plants. An adult requires about 330 pounds of food each day.

*E*lephants feed regularly. In the part of the forest near the Amboseli field where we were camping, one of the families would arrive very early each morning. The females rummage amongst the acacia branches for the tenderest twigs, which they break gently with their trunks and chew on them, thorns and all, without seeming to suffer. Right next to us, one female found nothing of interest to eat on the lower branches, so lengthened her trunk like a tentacle to reach up to the greenest, most inviting shoots. She was no acrobat like the large male we had met the evening before in the same area. We had come across him standing on his hind legs, stretched right up like a balancing artiste! This was how he managed to reach the highest branches of a parasol acacia, like a real connoisseur! Just thinking of such a heavy animal in that position is wearying, but he seemed quite at ease. He then came during the night to eat from the trees in our camp after he found a passage through the fence. Not even the strongest beam of light we pointed at him seemed to bother him, and he kept on eating calmly.

Another female pulled off a piece of bark from the tree behind us, using her tusks and trunk. The youngest elephants were unable to reach the branches and had to be content with picking up the twigs or bits of bark left by the adults. The whole family then came out of the forest and turned its attention to the tufts of grass in the field. In synchrony with its neighbor, each elephant unearthed a clump by pulling gently on the base with the end of its trunk and kicking gently with a front foot. Some who used their right tusk also preferred to use their right foot. Then they would beat the clump of grass against their foot to knock off the earth, then ferry it to their mouth. The same procedure would be carried out with the next clump while the previous one was still being chewed. As elephants need a great deal of food, the meal lasts a long time.

Toward eleven o'clock, the family headed toward the marsh where they ate large clusters of aquatic plants and papyrus. Everything is chewed conscientiously and at the same rhythm. When elephants pull up the root of a plant, they bite off only the edible section and leave the rest. Some plants sink their roots up to seven feet below the water level but that does not bother either the adults or the young, who are happy to submerge themselves up to their ears. In this way, they can feed themselves for hours in deep water, though the young have difficulty in following their elders in such circumstances. Occasionally, one finds itself with its head underwater and has to swim.

As the weeks passed, the lack of rain meant that the ground dried out. After a while the grass turned yellow and was no longer nourishing. As soon as the elephants came out from the forest, they headed straight for the marsh, no longer bothering with the grass on the savannah. All the elephants seemed sad, they no longer played or chased one another. The matriarch quickly entered the water, followed by her companions and their young. We waited all day but only saw them in the late afternoon. Observation became very difficult. On the following mornings, several of the families we had been watching regularly were absent, and we concluded that the drought had driven them to another part of the park.

The contrast between the wet and dry seasons was very marked. By the end of the dry season, the elephants became very thin; they ate without enthusiasm and the food gave them very little energy. Their movements were slow as if they were consciously economizing their strength. When the rains at last returned and the wind carried the smell of wet earth and fresh grass, the elephants pawed the ground and showed their excitement. Although they remained thin for a while longer, their behavior changed quickly and their movements were faster and livelier. The first time they found green grass, they ate it without pause, not even stopping to sleep at night! It had been many weeks, even months, since they last ate tasty, nourishing grass. From that moment on, they became playful, jokingly charging our vehicle and a tourist group's minibus. They followed one another, trumpeting and throwing clumps of grass, happily wasting their energy.

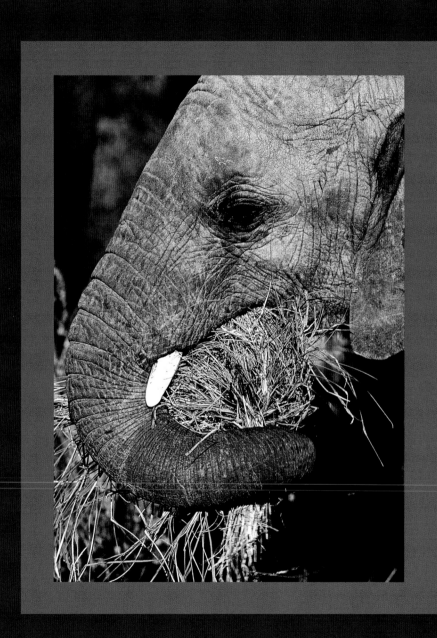

A BIG EATER

An animal of such large size has enormous daily food requirements. Whereas whales–the giants who inhabit the seas–simply open their mouths to filter the seawater and swallow the plankton it contains, elephants must make a constant physical effort, not just to find and take food, but also to chew, swallow and digest the plants that they need each day. In order to extract the juice from the fibers and to grind up the hard substances, elephants have evolved a physical apparatus suited to this function. Each of the two lower and upper half-jaws have only one molar, which is lined with diamond-shaped enamel ridges. The number of these ridges increases with the age of the animal. Although the ridges are very resistant, chewing causes progressive wear so old teeth are replaced with new ones. The tooth does not grow up from beneath the worn one, as occurs in other mammals, but behind it, pushing the old tooth horizontally forward until it falls out. Besides their milk teeth, elephants are born with the first two molars in each half-jaw. The first molar falls out at the age of 2 and the second, rather larger, around the age of 5. The third molar remains useable until the age of 10 or 12, and the fourth until the creature is 25 or 28. The fifth will remain until the animal reaches 45 or so, when the last will appear. This final one can last as long as 20 years. However, few elephants live that long and, in the wild, an elephant is unlikely to exceed 65 years of age.

At every change of teeth, the new one is larger than its predecessor and the number of ridges greater. In adult elephants, the molar can be the size of a brick (the crown measures 12 inches long and 2 inches wide) and weigh between 4 and 5 pounds. Fossils of mastodons reveal that this dentition has long existed but the mastodons' crowns did not have transversal folds of enamel surrounded by dentine, but rounded protrusions that probably were unable to grind large or hard plants. Therefore, their teeth were less efficient than those of elephants today.

The movements of a herd of elephants are determined by the search for food and water. In general, elephants are very regular in their eating and drinking habits. They dedicate up to 18 hours a day to this activity, which they only interrupt briefly for pauses during the day or for a few hours rest at night, during which even the adults lie down and sleep.

Elephants prefer seeds and fruit and some are happy to leave their reserves to enter villages to eat the mangoes! But they cannot be picky because an adult requires between 330 and 440 pounds of food a day. They feed on a variety of things: grass, leaves, fruit, tubercles, roots, bark, and even wood, which their powerful jaws can crush. They especially love the soft, succulent wood of the baobab, which they bite into deeply to extract the fiber. During the rainy season, elephants have a clear preference for grass. How they celebrate when the savannah begins to turn green once more is a sight to be seen!

These friendly giants do not need to lower their heads to see what there is to eat on the ground as their trunk tells them everything they need to know: the nature of the plant, its smell, and whether it is edible. Elephants are able to do several things at once, for example, graze as they walk, hold the food with their lower lip, and chew.

Dust showers are not restricted to bath time: every now and then, the females stop eating to spray themselves.

173
Like this male in musth, elephants are able to stand on their hind legs to reach the branches at a height of 20 feet from the ground.

When standing on their hind legs, with their bodies and trunks outstretched, adults can reach the shoots and fruit at up to 20 feet from the ground. Among land-based creatures, only the giraffe is capable of reaching higher.

Despite their great appetite, elephants are very cautious. They soften their food with the tip of their trunk before placing it in their mouth and always clean off the earth from roots by shaking the plant. They regularly eat bark but, unfortunately, this habit often causes fatal wounds to trees. Knocking down an acacia is child's play to an adult male: all he needs to do is to place his trunk on the bole and to shake it with all his strength; once the tree is down, he may enjoy the thorny parts. Experts, however, believe that only 2-3% of elephants have this habit.

Elephants are delicate creatures. These enormous eating machines require not only a large quantity of vegetation each day, but also a wide selection of plants that provide them with the principal minerals. If essential elements are missing from their diet, the animals rapidly weaken and this prompts them to travel to areas where water is always present. When this occurs, their nutrition generally worsens and, as they feel the effects of dietary deficiencies more quickly than other mammals, malnutrition quickly takes them into a lethargic but non-painful state caused by having too high a proportion of sugar in their blood. This happens when they still have food in their stomach but in insufficient quantities and, above all, when necessary nutritional elements are lacking. If the situation is prolonged, elephants become comatose, sleep for increasingly long periods, and are without the energy necessary to move away from

174
This animal is shaking a dum palm with all his strength to bring the fruit down; it is a favorite food of elephants.

175
A trunk can grasp a branch with as much precision as a human hand.

water. Inevitably, the moment arrives when they are no longer able to get up and they die rapidly.

The marshes and branches of the river offer ideal conditions for sick or wounded elephants to take refuge. There they find water and tender, easily chewed vegetation, even if it is not nutritional. These places are suitable for old animals whose last teeth have been worn down. All that is required, however, for the area to fill with the skeletons is for the water source to dry up in some manner or for a drought to occur. This, more than anything, has contributed to the legend about the Elephants' Graveyard, though, as we shall see, the myth is not entirely without foundation.

Elephants have a simple digestive system. The digestion process begins when food enters the creature's disproportionately small mouth. The saliva glands begin to operate, and the mucous glands in the short esophagus help to lubricate the coarse bundles of vegetation that make up much of the animal's diet. The simplicity of the digestive system is exemplified by the stomach, which is no more than a vertical bag whose principal function is to store food. It plays no role in digestion, which occurs mainly in the caecum. Larger than the stomach, the caecum contains a very rich intestinal flora that is necessary to absorb cellulose. The caecum also assimilates starch, glucides, and the albumin of certain plants.

Digestion can last from 22 to 46 hours, following which 40-60% of the food consumed leaves the intestine to be transformed. The grains and seeds are not transformed by the gastric juices and, when expelled, are the delight of small animals, insects,

birds and even baboons. The hundreds of pounds of excrement produced by an adult elephant are a perfect habitat for unabsorbed seeds, which germinate to form new plants. In this manner, elephants effectively plant the seeds of herbaceous and grasslike plants, shrubs and trees during their journeys, and often they carry the seeds far from the place where they were swallowed. It seems that the seeds of certain tropical forest trees and lianas are propagated purely by elephants, for example, the makorè (*Tieghemella heckelii*), an African tree whose hard, reddish wood is a popular export item. The tree is increasingly rare and only grows along elephant routes. And the seeds of the African apple tree–the size of a tennis ball–have only been found in elephant excrement as other animals do not eat them. The jaws of an elephant are capable of breaking the largest and hardest shells of any tropical fruit to free the seeds inside.

In the Samburu reserve, elephants are large consumers of the fruit of the dum palm, the seeds of which are sufficiently resistant to pass undamaged into the animal's stomach. In Manyara, the commonest tree is the flattish umbrella-thorn acacia whose yellow pods contain the seeds that elephants love; during the dry season elephants gorge themselves on them, shaking the trees with all their weight to make the pods fall.

It has been said that elephants are destructive to the environment in which they live, but their role in the regeneration of the forest by spreading the seeds of many plant species should not be forgotten. It seems, in fact, that the number of plant species is falling in the regions where elephants no longer live.

176 and 177
In the Amboseli marshes, the elephants feed on
enormous bundles of papyrus and other plants.
When plants come up with roots attached, they
eat the plants and leave the earth-filled roots.

178
During the dry season, savannah elephants
spend a great deal of time in Amboseli marshes.
They arrive in the early morning and sometimes
remain until after dark.

179
Forest elephants are less well known than their
grassland cousins. They prefer the recesses of the
damp forests for their nourishment and bathing.

180 and 181
The abundance of food allows this adolescent to
take time to play with tufts of grass. He has
played with these 'trophies' for more than an
hour.

182
Face to face, two females eat peacefully. Half of the plants swallowed are thrown up before being digested.

183
Forest elephants are easily recognized by their straight, slender tusks. Like their savannah relatives, they eat with constant attention, choosing the most succulent leaves.

THWARTED MIGRATION

184
A matriarch guides her herd toward better pasture. A group of elephants can walk up to 30 miles a day at a speed of 4 miles an hour.

185
In certain periods of the year, different 'allied' herds meet in a large clan in which social intercourse plays a very important role.

186
During movement across the savannah, the young have to adapt to the speed of the herd.

187
Studies have shown that a particular group of cattle egrets always follows the same family of elephants. Moving elephants disturb insects from grass or branches. The egrets, which are waders, feed on the flying insects.

185

At the start of the 20th century, when more than 5 million elephants lived in Africa, no one thought that they represented a threat to the ecosystem in which they roamed. Today, though there are no more than a few hundred thousand across the entire continent, they can cause serious damage. The problem is the restrictions imposed by the reserves in which they are confined. At one time, before Europeans arrived in Africa, elephants used their habitat on a cyclical basis. Their migrations were based on the search for new grazing land, like those the gnu today in the Serengeti and Masai-Mara parks. Elephants exploited the resources of a region and, when these had been exhausted, moved on and did not return for several years. Even if they uprooted trees, the damage, though spectacular, did not have lasting consequences as they were spread widely across time and space. Their impact on the countryside was even considered positive, as they placed vegetation that was otherwise inaccessible within the reach of small herbivores, and they even created paths through thick savannah.

Today, however, such migrations have been made impossible. Inhabited zones mostly surround the national parks, and the elephants are now unable to leave their sanctuaries. For these large, intelligent, wandering consumers, the problems caused by the situation are acute and have arisen more quickly than for any other herbivorous species. The elephants' surprising memory for places and events means they are easily able to distinguish between areas where they are left in peace and those where they are persecuted. The negative impact they have on their environment is the result of the limitations of the spaces in which they are imprisoned.

In Amboseli, for example, elephants have always understood the periods of drought and abundance and have migrated accordingly. Now, such movements to new grazing land have become very difficult owing to the Kenyan government's decision to settle the Masai people. The elephants are therefore forced to move during the dry season to the foot of Kilimanjaro where the vegetation stays green, with the result that the resources of the park are being exploited at an unsustainable level.

DRINKING

*188 left
An adolescent male plays in
a pool of mud.*

*188 right
Excellent swimmers,
elephants can cross deep
rivers and even stretches of
sea.*

*190 and 191
Playfulness reaches new
heights of intensity at
bathing time, and not even
the adolescents and females
(right) can resist joining in
the make-believe combat.*

At Samburu the families of elephants generally pass the night in the hills so that each morning we have to wait while they descend to the river. For this reason we take up a position on the plain that gives us a wide view. The herds do not meet each morning in the same place, and on occasion it is impossible to follow them as the vegetation is too thick. The elephants generally appear between 8 and 9 a.m., and it is very unusual for them to go to drink before that time, but today we are lucky and the first family comes into sight at 7.30. They eat peacefully, close to us, as two other families appear in the distance. Suddenly, the matriarch decides that the moment has come to drink and leads the entire group quickly into the water, leaving us just enough time to arrange ourselves where we can see them without causing a disturbance.

The first females reach the sandy riverbank and dip the ends of their trunks into the water. They lift their heads a little and then raise their trunks to their mouths and let the water run down their throats. Two calves prefer to kneel on the bank to drink while the adolescents walk into the deeper water; one submerges itself and its companions follow suit. The babies hurry to join them, one climbing on the shoulders of a neighbor, and another, the very youngest, holding its trunk above the water level as though it were a periscope. Playtime has begun and the joy they take in the water bursts out. One of the adolescents stands up and begins to run, sending up great spurts of water, then the mothers decide that they too want to play and join in with the younger generation. The movement, noise and sprays of water become intense. Two young females lock tusks and push, and a second family arrives to drink and join those already in the water. The two families greet one another, then the games begin once more.

The first matriarch crosses the river, followed by her companions, but the adolescents have no desire to leave the water and hang back. On the other side of the river the bank is steep and muddy. The females pound the mud with their feet, then suck it up with their trunks and spray it over their shoulders, backs and stomachs. Finally, the adolescents arrive but they prefer to roll in the mud and spread it over their heads, ears and eyes. Then they stand, sit down again and let themselves roll over onto the others. The smaller ones take advantage of this to climb on top of their elders. Eventually, they all leave the quagmire they have created and slip and slide as they climb up the bank. With difficulty they reach the top, where the females are waiting for them.

The second group is still in the water, but at the bend further down the river, a third family crosses to our side. An old male comes down to drink and, for a moment, he lifts his trunk to sniff the air in the direction of the females. Those in the river leave the water and enter the forest on the other side, but the male is not interested in joining them and wanders off in the direction from which he arrived. In the end, we find ourselves alone as the families eat on the other bank.

192
A baby just a few weeks old bathes under the watchful eye of his mother. The young do not seem to be afraid of water and soon learn to swim, helped by their trunks.

193
A female elephant and her youngster cross the river in search of better vegetation. Despite the apparent greenness of the banks, the dry season brings little food.

WATER, THE FOUNT OF LIFE

Elephants must have water. Whether the source is a lake, a permanent pool or a spring, they will track it down. To find water they will even dig down into a dry riverbed. Using their tusks and feet, they can dig holes of more than a meter in depth, then, with their trunks, they can filter the water they find in the subsoil. These holes are then used by other animals that, without the presence of elephants, would otherwise have no access to water. In general, adult elephants drink between 20 and 26 gallons of water a day, and even more if they have been forced to go without for a few days. They also need water with which to bathe and cool themselves. The prospect of a good bathe during the dry season prompts herds to travel more than 20 miles.

Plant juice can slake the thirst of an elephant for a day or two, but then water becomes essential. The small population of elephants that lives in the Namibian Desert has adapted perfectly to the harshness of the environment, having developed genetic characteristics like the strange ability to locate water in the middle of nowhere. They eat frugally from the trees and shrubs in the region and are able to go without drinking for 3 or 4 days, even after traveling long distances. On their journeys between water sources, they eat plants that are completely unsuited to other animals. In the savannah, elephants drink whenever they can, once a day or sometimes even twice during the height of the dry season. They love fresh, clear water like pools of fresh rainwater.

Paradoxically, they are the first to pollute springs by defecating or urinating in them, or even by churning up the mud when they bathe. Normally, the herds go to drink and cool themselves in the middle of the day or the evening. There are many elephants living on the islands in the delta of the river Okavango in Botswana. When they exhaust the resources on one island, they move to another, often by swimming. Elephants are good swimmers even though they do not float very easily; they keep the top of their heads above water and stick their trunks up like a nozzle.

In the forest, where there is no lack of water, each time they cross a river or stream, they drink a small quantity of water. Compared to elephants that live in the desert, the life of forest elephants is almost amphibious.

To drink, elephants only use their trunk. They dip it in the water and suck the liquid up (a maximum of 2.5 gallons), hold it there, then blow it out again into their mouth. When they have had enough, they spray their head and body, then lie down in the water. Only the youngest, who still have not learned to use their trunks, kneel to drink directly with their mouths.

194

*When water is close, elephants frequently break
into a run to reach it quickly.*

195

*This family is faithful to its habits: almost every
morning they arrive on the bank of the Ewaso
Ngiro in Samburu, between 9 and 11 a.m.*

196
*It's bath time: surrounded by spray and
trumpeting, this young elephant seems impatient
to get to the deeper water and immerse himself.*

197
*Having reached one of the few water sources in
East Tsavo during the dry season, an elephant
charges the buffaloes to clear the bank.*

198 top
The egrets are always ready to take advantage
of the presence of elephants. As they cross the
marshes, the elephants scatter frogs and toads
into the open, where they become part of the
birds' diet.

198 bottom
Completely immersed, a young elephant uses its
trunk as a snorkel.

199
Having reached the marshes in the early
morning, usually around 8 to 9 a.m., the
families move off into the most favorable
areas and begin to feed. The young are
never left alone.

200 and 201
The marshes are a safe refuge for the
elderly, sick or wounded as water is
available and the plants are more easily
chewed than those of the savannah.

202
This youngster eats earth mixed with sand to benefit from their minerals.

203 top
In the savannah the elephants drink once, perhaps twice, a day, generally heading off to the water reserves in the mid-morning or late afternoon.

203 bottom
The river is not very deep, so even the small elephants have to lie down to immerse themselves.

204 and 205
Bath time is a special time for the whole herd, but to the matriarch alone belongs the choice of the moment to enter the water.

206

The herd has chosen a pool to wallow in. Once out of the mud, the excited adolescents begin to play.

207

This female is gathering sand from a bank, and will sprinkle herself with it.

208

After the bathe, the elephants often cover themselves with dust. It sticks to their skin and creates a protective layer against insects.

209

Dust is also an abrasive which allows the animals to keep their skin healthy.

ELEPHANTS — DRINKING

DUST AND MUD BATHS

Using their trunk, elephants cover themselves with dust several times a day. This bath is generally carried out at the same time as other social activities, especially when close to water. The layer of dust almost always covers existing layers of dried mud and tends to color the animals gray or red–as in Tsavo in Kenya–depending on the type of soil. Elephants love to roll on clayey banks and in mud pools, especially the younger members of the herd, but the elders also cover themselves with dark, sticky mud, picking it up in the curve of their trunk and throwing it onto their shoulders, back, flanks, head and chest. Why do they do it? Firstly, it is a source of pleasure, but, at a practical level, it provides a layer of protection against the heat. Having originally lived in forests, elephants use various methods to combat excessive heat, such as fanning themselves with their ears and protecting their skin from the sun with layers of mud and dust. A side effect is that these layers also aid to protect the skin against parasites or the stings of mosquitoes, tsetse flies and other insects. Unlike other large herbivores, elephants do not like "cleaner" birds like the cattle egrets, which are very effective in picking off impurities or nesting insects from the skin. This intolerance partly explains why elephants spray themselves so readily with water, mud, dust. The young, who have not yet learned to use their trunks for this purpose, roll on the ground or are sprayed by their mothers.

The digestive system of elephants is not very effective and thus they suffer from stomach ache. To alleviate this problem, they regularly visit saltpans where they dig into the ground with their tusks, trunk or front feet and turn the earth into a fine dust, which they suck up. The earth is impregnated with sodium chloride but also with calcium, phosphorus, magnesium, iron and kaolin, and this last substance helps relieve their stomach pains. The elephant's organism absorbs all the sodium in the saltpan which helps to eliminate the excess of toxic potassium that exists in its feed. The calcium aids in the growth of tusks, so that elephants living near saltpans are often endowed with large incisors. So that they can more easily reach the salt, the females kneel on the ground in the same way that the young elephants kneel to eat directly with their mouths. When several families visit such areas at the same time, the wait to take up station in the saltpan depends on the status of the arriving matriarch. If the group of a high-ranking female arrives when others are feeding, the lower ranking group will move away at the first sign of a threat. Elephants are also happy to destroy termite mounds just to take advantage of the rich soil the termites create.

Some saltpans are temporary, while others have been frequented by elephants for thousands of years. For example, they used to visit the caves on Mount Elgon in Kenya (which reaches a height of 14,100 feet) for their salt. This ancient volcano has a large number of caves where the El Gonyi tribe of Masai once lived. As a matter of caution, the elephants visited the caves only by night, following a precise path that was handed down over the generations and moving over landslips with great caution. To satisfy their needs, they used to dig into the walls with their tusks and the marks are still visible. Today the herds no longer visit the caves. Might it be because the matriarchs are no longer capable to leading them there?

210 top
A cloud of dust rises around an elephant that
has just completed sprinkling itself with sand.

210 bottom
The adults usually use their trunk to sprinkle
themselves with earth, whereas the inexpert
youngsters are obliged to roll over in the clay on
the banks.

211
Once dry, the layer of mud accumulated during
the mud bath is eliminated with vigorous shaking.

212 and 213
Rolling in the mud is necessary for health
reasons, but is also a pleasure in itself and one
of the many playful activities in which elephants
indulge.

214 and 215
The activity of covering oneself with water, sand
or mud is not instinctual but part of an
elephant's education. This very young male,
seen here in the marshes of Musiara, learns
partly through imitation, but above all by means
of his mother's active help.

216 and 217
The trunk nebulizes mud in a very efficient and
versatile manner as it is able to reach the elephant's
head, back and even the stomach.

218 and 219
Storms have left many mud-filled puddles. In the torrid
heat, two males take advantage of them to cover their
bodies with mud.

220
A young male follows his mother into the safe
environment of the marshes, accompanied by
cattle egrets.

PHOTOGRAPHIC CREDITS